Watching the Road is bea[...] [...]-
wavering faith and a mot[...] a
transformed life . . . my li[...] 1
because of the hope and prayers of this story. Prayer changes things,
and like this book perfectly depicts, NOTHING is impossible with
God! Keep hoping, keep believing, keep watching the road, and never give up hope for your loved one's return! Your prodigal could be
just over the horizon!

Lindsey Doss
Co-Pastor of Hope Unlimited Church, Author of *The Way Home*
Knoxville, Tennessee

. . . .

I have known Karen and Rick for many years. Honestly, I don't know
of two people who have endured so many sudden attacks from the
enemy in their families, ministry, and business. While most believ-
ers would have lain down, rolled over, and just quit, they have endured. My wife, Pam, and I have watched their unwavering faith.
What I like the most about this book is that it is not written by
someone with Bible knowledge only or as some self-help spiritual
manual. Karen has written from both knowledge and experience.
She has proven the Word of God works and has shown that faith and
patience—the power twins of the Kingdom—will undergird your
weakest moments and become your "Aaron" and "Hur" to hold you
up until the victory is won. What God has done for Karen and Rick,
He can and will do for you.

Perry Stone
Founder of V.O.E., I.S.O.W., and O.C.I.
Cleveland, Tennessee

In this powerful book, *Watching the Road*, you will gain crucial revelation that has been tested in the crucible of experience. It is a direct result of our Faithful Father and the tenacity of a mother who refused to be refused. Find hope in this book to never give in, never give up, and never lose hope. Never lose faith, your miracle is coming down the road.

Judy Jacobs Tuttle
Co-Pastor of Dwelling Place Church International, Psalmist/Author
Cleveland, Tennessee

. . . .

Karen tells a story in which you can picture the scenes, sense the scents, imagine the sounds, and feel the emotions. The story is told just that well. But there's more than a story here. There's a heartfelt, gut-wrenching, soul-searching pursuit of promise and hope. There's a God who hears and answers. Hope becomes embodied in flesh. And through it all, you'll learn how to fight for the prodigal in your family for whom you long.

Bob Sorge
Author of *Secrets of the Secret Place*
Kansas City, Missouri

. . . .

Karen Wheaton is a hero of mine. She stayed true to hope in a season of deep pain, and the victory she received on the other side was nothing short of a true miracle. The words written in these pages have cost her much. *Watching the Road* is a must read. This story of tenacious faith and trust in God and His promises will encourage you no matter what season of life you may find yourself."

Havilah Cunnington
Founder of Truth to Table
Author of *Stronger Than the Struggle*
Redding, California

Watching the Road is based on a very specific testimony—a miracle that Karen rightly identifies as the most powerful miracle she has ever witnessed (and believe me, Karen has seen lots of miracles). Such a miracle is not reserved for the few and fortunate; it is the inheritance of every single believer in Jesus. *Watching the Road* shares Karen's very transparent story of how prayer and intercession got her through a period of true "hell on Earth." Not only does she share her story, but she personally mentors you on how to pray UNTIL prayers, based on what she learned going through the trenches and coming out on the other side.

Larry Sparks, MDiv.
Publisher, Destiny Image
Author of *Breakthrough Faith* and compiler of *Ask for the Rain*
Lawrencesparks.com

. . . .

We have known Karen and Rick for many years and have the distinct privilege of serving on the board of directors for the Ramp. From this place of service, we have been able to observe not only the broken place of a prodigal daughter but the resilient faith of a godly mother. It's been life-changing for us to witness such a tenacious pursuit of the Presence of God and to see His power restore all that was lost. As you read *Watching the Road*, we believe you will walk away as we have: challenged, convicted, encouraged, and inspired, along with a fresh view of the beauty and depth of God's unfailing love and faithfulness!

Rusty and Leisa Nelson
Lead Pastors of The Rock Family Worship Center
Huntsville, Alabama

WATCHING THE ROAD

PRAYING YOUR PRODIGAL HOME

KAREN WHEATON

*I dedicate this book to
my Heavenly Father.
He kept every promise.*

ACKNOWLEDGMENTS

. . . .

Special thanks to:

Lindsey and Casey,
Thank you for your yes to God and to each other. Though costly, it is beautiful to see the reward of your obedience. Thank you for allowing me to share your story so others can experience the miracle of restoration in their own lives. You are my joy and crown.

My husband, Rick Towe,
Thank you for giving me the freedom to spend so much of my life on the front porch, not only for the sake of our own children, but for the wayward sons and daughters of this generation. You sacrificed much so that this book could be written. I love you in every way.

Lauren and Samuel Bentley,
We lived this story together, the pain and the tears, and now we share the joy of the miracle. Your love and strength were there for me to lean on, then and now. Thank you for your faithfulness to God and the mission He has given us. You are my gift and reward.

My mother, Nell Harris,
Thank you for helping me write this book with your example of what love and faith look like every day of your life. I love you.

My sister, Janet Alexander,
We shared the memories of the valley and the miracle of this story.
God gave me one sister . . . I'm glad it was you.

Edie Mourey,
You are a gift from God to my life. You made the challenge of writing this story a joy, awakening in me a love for writing. Thank you.

Front Porch Friends,
You know who you are, and more importantly the Father knows. You were there, right beside me, praying, decreeing, pacing, believing, encouraging me, and watching with me. I am eternally grateful. Now, we rejoice together, "For this daughter of mine was dead, and now has returned to life. She was lost, and now she is found. Let the party begin!" (Luke 15:24).

CONTENTS

"Please, Lindsey, don't take this path. It will destroy your life. I'm begging you to listen to me!"

Uncomfortable and anxious, she sat in the chair, arms folded, eyes dark. Finally, she spoke, "You cannot tell me God's will for my life. No one can tell me that!"

"But, Lindsey, God's will for our lives has already been laid out for us in His Word! I'm only telling you what He has already made clear for us!"

For an hour and a half, I poured out my heart and my love with everything in me and every way I knew how. There were moments I thought she was possibly hearing me—moments I thought I could see the slightest movement of her heart toward the truth that was so evident. Now, it was time for the conversation to be over. I'd try one more time to bring her back to the truth and back to her family. Everything in me was hoping and praying this would be the instant she'd come to her senses and have a change of heart.

Chapter One

.....

THE VIEW FROM
THE PORCH

What do you do when someone you love changes into someone you've never known? What do you do when you are watching her make decisions you know will destroy her life? What do you say when everything you try to say falls on deaf ears and only widens the gap between you? How do you hold on and let go at the same time?

Luke 15:11–32 tells us the story of a father who was faced with these same questions. His youngest son decided he wanted to go his own way. He wanted freedom from the perceived prison of his father's home. The son couldn't wait for his father to die so that he could receive his inheritance. He wanted it right then. Knowing the decisions the son was making could cost him his very soul, his father released him to go.

Even though the story doesn't reveal a lot about the father, many of us who have been in his place believe we know him quite well. We understand how he felt when he withdrew the inheritance he had spent most of his life preserving. Knowing it would be squandered, the father placed it in the hands of a son who didn't care if his dad lived or died. We have felt the deep pain of the father's soul as his son turned to walk away. We have experienced the father's miserable sleepless nights. We have identified with the challenge of trying to carry on the responsibilities that life required of him with one thought continually on the forefront of his mind—*Where is my son?!*

There is another place I have shared with this father: his front porch. It was here he learned the secret that would eventually bring his son back home: *True love lets go; true faith holds on.*

Days turned to weeks, weeks to months, months to years. There were no signs of hope. There were no letters, no emails, no phone calls. It mattered not. Every day, the father stood on the porch with eyes of faith and a heart of hope, watching the road.

Grandmother's Front Porch

I live in my grandmother's house. It sits beside Williams Creek in a beautiful valley in Northwestern Alabama, surrounded by hills and blue skies. Next to the house stands the Millhouse overlooking the roaring dam that my grandfather designed and built in the 1940s.

My grandmother and grandfather have been in Heaven now for a number of years. They built this house themselves in 1935 for three hundred dollars! My mother and her only brother spent their childhood years inside this house. Grandmother held many a prayer meeting and home church service in its little living room. Even my great grandmother was often in those meetings and prayer gatherings. Her name was Molly Lolley. She was known as a woman of prayer and great faith. When you include my own children, these walls have held the sounds of the worship, songs, and prayers of five generations. I spent most of my own childhood here. I would rather have been here than any place on Earth.

All summer, my sister, Janet, and I swam in the creek and fished for bass and brim. The ancient bluffs were for exploring and digging for Native treasures. But there was one place that brought it all together—the front porch. The front porch bridged the joy and wonders of the outside to the warmth and love on the inside.

On the front porch, Grandmother's swing still hangs in the same place it was when I sat beside her and listened to her sing to me. I can still hear her singing, "Hush little baby, don't say a word, Daddy's gonna buy you a mockingbird." It was so peaceful there, pressed up against her as close as I could get. She was a little extra "fluffy," so it made it all the better.

The front porch was simple with a concrete floor and a wooden ceiling that Grandpa painted sky blue. Grandpa was also a welder, so he had fashioned and placed the post himself. Climbing up one side of the post was the beautiful rose bush that Grandmother had planted. She loved roses. There was usually a birdhouse or two that sat on top of the post that was filled with little baby birds each spring—barn swallows, I think.

There was a concrete sidewalk that led up to the front porch. It was lined with buttercups in early spring. It stretched out to the main road, welcoming visitors who might want to come by and sit awhile, or family who wanted to come home.

The edge of the porch was often used for fine dining—country style, that is. Grandpa would bring a freshly picked watermelon from the garden, take out his pocket knife, and slice it open. He always gave me the "heart" of the melon, because he knew it was my favorite. It tasted like the sweet kiss of a grandfather's love.

Shaded by a huge pecan tree, the edge of the porch was also where Grandmother stood, pointing over the hill toward the southwestern skyscape, teaching Janet and me to watch out for tornadoes. She let us help her look for impending trouble clouds. We learned to pay attention to times when the disturbed atmosphere made the air thick and balmy and the sky a yellow greenish hue.

As the sun went down on the summer nights, the front porch became a front-row seat to the bullfrog and cricket choir concert occasioned by the whip-poor-will repeating its own name. Every evening, their mesmerizing rhythms calmed the soul, causing the cares of life to melt into a peaceful bliss. And the scent of the twining honeysuckle, fragrant four o'clocks, and perfumed petunias round about the porch infused the air.

As a child, it seemed as though time stood still on that front porch. It seemed as though Grandmother and Grandpa would always be there with open arms and loving smiles. But I was wrong.

Before I realized what was happening, time was changing everything. The little girl who was captured by the wonders in the valley began to wonder about what was outside the valley.

As a child, I had begun to sing in church, and by the time I was a teenager, I began to feel the stirring of an unquenchable desire to travel and sing. At the age of seventeen, I was accepted into a school of ministry in Fort Mill, South Carolina. Life was moving quickly. I packed my bags, loaded my car, and prepared to head out on a new adventure that would lead me far away from the valley and the front porch I had shared with my grandmother.

Before I left, I had to go back to see her again. She listened to me as I shared with her my dream of ministry. Her brown eyes held a mixture of emotions—excitement, concern, deep love, and a little sadness. With a heartfelt embrace, I said goodbye, got into my car, and began to slowly pull out of the gravel drive. With a quick glance into my rearview mirror, my heart melted into tears as the mirror became a frame to hold the memories and the image of the front porch I so loved.

Once again, though only for a moment, time stood still, leaving me with a snapshot that would stay with me for the rest of my life. It was Grandmother, slowly swinging in her swing, alone, watching me leave. Eternity was beckoning her and a call from God was beckoning me.

A Home in the Making

The road that led me out of the valley had some unexpected turns and detours I never imagined I would have to take. Only three years later, I was married and traveling in full-time ministry, singing and sharing the message of the Gospel—just like I had dreamed. Within two years, God had given us a beautiful, blond-headed, blue-eyed girl with dimples. We named her Lauren. Grandmother called her Tootle.

I remember the first time I brought my little baby bundle up the steps of the front porch and placed her in Grandmother's arms. I wanted Lauren to know Grandmother and love her as I had. I wanted Lauren to share the swing, the songs, the sights, and the sounds of the porch that I had known as a child. But it wasn't to be. Grandmother's time with Lauren lasted only two short years.

On the day my grandmother died, we left the hospital and gathered at her house to be together as a family. My mother had taken Lauren and arrived at the house ahead of me. When I pulled into the driveway, I noticed my grandfather, my dad, and many others standing on the front porch. I saw my mother walking toward me with a panicked look on her face. Then I saw the large lump on Lauren's forehead. She had fallen on the steps of the front porch and went down face first, leaving a huge goose egg above her brow. I scooped her into my arms and headed for the emergency room. All turned out well. It was just a sad memory of a sad day.

Only a year later, God gave us another precious little girl we called Lindsey. I remember the first time I looked into her dark blue eyes and smiled at her thick curly black hair. She was everything I dreamed she would be.

Although our life was good, it certainly wasn't without its challenges. I did my best to shield the girls from the fact that the marriage between their father and me was slowly falling apart. After almost thirteen years of trying my best to hold onto a marriage that was riddled with infidelity, it ended in divorce. As a young, naïve, Southern Pentecostal girl, it was the turn in the road I had never envisioned. I believed marriage was forever. After all, my parents were married for sixty years, both sets of my grandparents were married over fifty years each. And not a one of Grandma Lolley's twelve children she raised ever divorced.

During those years, I learned a lot about the deep pain of betrayal, the process of forgiveness, and the power of God to heal and restore. It was out of this place of brokenness that I stood in amazement as God brought a wonderful man into my life to fulfill His promise to heal and restore my heart. Not only was the man extremely handsome, he had a wholehearted love for God. His name was Rick Towe. A very close ministry friend named Perry Stone had introduced us and had told me, "He said he would treat you like a queen!" Known as a man of loyalty, character, and integrity, Rick Towe has kept his word. We were married in a small private ceremony. His gentleness of heart and spirit brought healing to the girls and me.

Rick was a "city boy." Well, he's from Chattanooga, Tennessee. But being from an Alabama town of six thousand people, most of whom are kin to me, I considered Chattanooga to be a "big city"! Since his job was in the city, it only made sense for us to live there as we formed our new family. We had a beautiful home, in a beautiful city, but there was only one problem: The valley kept calling me home.

I tried to like the city life. Really, I did.

The shopping was wonderful, and I love to shop.

The restaurants were amazing, and I love to eat.

But the subdivision we lived in, with all its gorgeous homes and manicured lawns, started to feel so confining.

I wanted the open spaces of Grandpa's pastures.

I wanted to walk down the old dirt road that runs behind my grandmother's house.

I needed to see the Little Dipper and the shooting stars at night.

I wanted my girls to know more than malls and manicures.

I wanted them to know what the woods smelled like, to discover the simple joys of shucking corn and shelling butter beans, and to be okay with getting their fingernails a little dirty.

But more than anything, I could not shake this unsettled sense in my spirit. Somehow, I felt this "pull" to go back home to Hamilton was bigger than I and my own preferences. It seemed as though God Himself was stirring something deep-seated in my soul that I did not understand.

After Rick would leave for the office, and the girls had been taken to school, my living room in Chattanooga would become a sanctuary, a place where I met with God. I had to have answers to what I was feeling and why I was feeling it.

Logically speaking, this made no sense. Rick's job was there. *What would he say if I dared to tell him what was happening inside me?* I wondered.

I continued to pray about this crazy thought. Pounding my fist on the end table beside my couch, one day, I began to wrestle with God, "Please tell me if this is really what You want. God, if this is You, help Rick to understand and desire the same thing!"

Finally, I could hold it in no longer. Later on, I tearfully poured out my heart to Rick about what I was hearing in my spirit. With no resistance from him whatsoever, he and I answered the call. We moved back to Hamilton, Alabama.

Rick decided it would be best for him to commute between the two cities as long as was necessary—working in Chattanooga during the week and driving to Hamilton on the weekends. Even though the sacrifice would be great, somehow, we knew it was right.

It had been exactly twenty years since I pulled out of Grandmother's driveway to follow my dream. Now, I was returning to the valley with Rick, two teenage girls, and a lot of lessons learned.

My parents had built a house right across the street from my grandparents' home. When we returned, they decided to downsize and allow us to move into their home. It was a perfect place for my girls to spend their teen years, and it gave me a perfect view of the front porch of the place that housed my happiest memories.

My Front Porch

After my grandmother died, my grandfather lived in the house alone for ten years. With Grandmother gone, the valley was never quite the same. Then, after Grandpa passed, the house sat empty for another ten years. I could hardly bear seeing the front porch look so lonely and lifeless.

All too quickly, my two girls had grown into young ladies who were ready for marriage and lives of their own. When Lindsey was engaged, I thought of a way that my grandmother's house could live again.

I decided to purchase the property from my mother and remodel the house for Lindsey and Casey, her new husband, to live in. Even though I made many changes inside the house, I felt the comforting love of my grandparents, knowing their hands had built the structure underneath the "new" that held it all together.

I painted Grandmother's swing and hung it back right where she had it. I left the sidewalk as it was, kind of broken up in a few places and rather worn from all the feet that had followed its leading to the front porch.

Lindsey and Casey spent the first year of their marriage in that house and on that porch. When their children came, they felt the house was too small, so they moved about a mile down the road. It was then I decided to make the house my own.

It's kind of funny, now as a mother and grandmother, I often find myself sitting on this same front porch, in my grandmother's swing, with my own grandchildren, singing the same songs Grandmother sang to me. When I am stressed, it is still the place I want to be.

Over the years, when I find myself in a fight for rest or when pressure steals my sleep, I envision myself as a little girl, sitting beside Grandmother in the swing. It takes me away to a time when life was simple and cares were few. I'm glad that place of her peaceful love is still alive in me.

It was also on this front porch I watched Lindsey walk out as she was leaving her husband and her family.

It was on this front porch I saw a broken-hearted Casey stand knocking on my door, needing comfort and counsel.

It was on this front porch that I stood as I was in prayer, shouting from the top of my lungs, "*Lindsey*! Come back to God!"

On this front porch, I often paced, from one end to the other, calling on the God of my mother and grandmothers, that He would bring my daughter home.

On January 10, 2016, it was this front porch that Lindsey walked across when she came to the door to tell me she was coming home.

Chapter Two

·····

THE STORM

Life had been good for Lindsey. In fact, she loved the life we lived as a family in full-time ministry, traveling across the nation in our black Silver Eagle bus and ministering with some of the greatest Christian leaders and ministers of our day. She enjoyed being around so many different people, the outgoing child she was.

When she wasn't with me on the road, she was living a child-hood dream back in Hamilton with my parents, Papaw Bill and Mama Nell. She spent time riding the tractor and trapping rac-coons with Papaw Bill, all the while being nurtured and cared for by Mama Nell. And her older sister, Lauren, was the perfect companion for her everyday life.

Lindsey was a girl full of life and joy, and she loved everybody. In fact, in elementary school, she won "The Most Loving" award for three years straight! She took delight in life and lived in an in-nocent wonder of the world around her. It made being around her a sheer pleasure as her positivity was, in fact, infectious.

But I would be fooling myself not to acknowledge that the frac-turing of my first marriage had no effect on her. Things happen in life—good and bad. And we all respond or react to them in our individual ways.

In Lindsey's case, below the surface, not visible to anyone, including her, a fissure had formed. Hurt, anger, confusion, disappointment, disillusionment—any weighty, emotionally-charged experience could flex and stress the cracking of her inner self. Yet all remained unseen to us and the outside world. Therefore, we couldn't foresee what was going to break out in Lindsey's life.

A Stirring Begins

It was a September night, only a few weeks after we had relocated, and I was driving in from a ministry trip. It was late, about 1:30 in the morning, when I made it to downtown Hamilton. Though I was eager to get home, something caught my eye. I looked to my left, and there they were—a group of young people sitting on the hoods of their parked cars. I was gripped with the thought, *They have no idea who the real God is, and they are just wasting their time.*

Suddenly, I heard God say, "I want you to work with the youth of this city."

"I'm too old, God. I'm not cool, and I'm busy in the ministry," was my response, or I should say, excuse.

Then God made me an offer He knew I would not be able to refuse: *"But what you invest in the lives of other young people, you'll reap in your children."*

At the time, Lauren was fifteen, and Lindsey was twelve. Since they were in those "challenging" years, I knew I would need all the help I could get, so without a clue of what was about to happen, I said, "Yes."

My sister, Janet, and her husband, Skip Alexander, pastored a small storefront church in the middle of downtown Hamilton. I decided the best way to "work with the youth of this community" would be to join their youth service on a Wednesday night when I wasn't on the road in ministry.

Maybe I can take some brownies or cookies in and just be a part of their service, I thought.

Sitting in the small, windowless, cinderblock room that first Wednesday night, with about seven young people (including Lauren and Lindsey), I fell in love with a generation. Their need and hunger were so evident. I knew I could help them find what would fill their empty, longing hearts. I didn't know all the cool "youth stuff" to do, and I wasn't interested in taking them on trips to Six Flags, but I knew this: I could love these kids and show them the way to the Presence of God.

Given the opportunity, I began to teach them about the "real God," and about His plan and purpose for their lives. Most important of all, I taught them the secret I had discovered as a young child: If you pray and seek Him, He will come.

Most of the youth didn't know how to pray, so I taught them by praying aloud and with all my heart. Needless to say, they stared awkwardly at me, but this was how I wanted to hear them pray one day. Quickly, their tender hearts responded. They began to express their hearts to God, and He answered their passionate prayers. He came! And when He came, the kids who were addicted to drugs didn't want the drugs anymore. Young men and women bound by sexual perversion wanted to live their lives in purity. Then these young ones went back to get their friends. Soon seven kids turned to thirty.

We outgrew the cinderblock room at the church and began meeting in a room above my garage. But that also became too small, so I rented a room in the shopping center by the church. We called it *The Grace Place.*

God was there. You could tell something supernatural was happening. I fell in love with these kids. I began to take them on the road with me as a ministry team called Chosen.

Within a year, I bought an old grocery store and converted it to a conference center. We began holding our youth services and conferences there. As I was trying to think of a new name for our conferences, I said to my daughter, "What do you think we should call it, Lauren? It's kind of like a rally, and it's kind of like a camp."

Lauren quickly responded, "It's a *Ramp!*" And *The Ramp* was born.

Several months later, as I was thumbing through the pages of a landscaping book, I ran across the definition of a ramp. It said that a ramp is a platform taking you from one level to another. I thought, *That's it! That's why it's called The Ramp! We are called to take these young men and women from where they are and launch them into the purposes of God for their lives.*

I learned a valuable lesson the night I heard the Voice as I watched a group of kids sitting on the hoods of their cars. It's this: *You never know what's behind your yes.*

Little did I know, I was answering a call that would bring tens of thousands of young men and women from around the world to the corner of Northwest Alabama to encounter the Presence of the real God. From that simple *yes* came a church, a school of ministry, and a promise from God that I would desperately need in the days to come.

Before the Storm

The encounter of the youth in the Grace Place days pulled a young man named Casey Doss out of the woods of a nearby community called Brilliant, Alabama. I remember the first time I saw him.

A friend had suggested I invite this young man to the Grace Place to preach. He had a hunger and passion for God that was very unusual and contagious.

Casey soon became a part of Chosen and a part of my heart. I loved him like a son. It was obvious that the touch of God was on his life. His character and integrity ran deep.

Lindsey, while in her early teen years, not long after we began our work in Hamilton, had begun to make unwise choices in her attempt to fill her need for relational acceptance. I had attributed it to the strained relationship she had had with her father. We did work to deal with these issues and seemed to find our way through them. I had prayed for a few years that, even though she was still quite young, God would send His perfect will for her life. I was thrilled, then, when I saw the spark of first love between Lindsey and Casey. I trusted Casey. He was wise beyond his years, but most of all, he walked with God. I felt confident he would love and protect her. With great joy and my blessing, Casey and Lindsey were married on February 14, 2005.

My oldest daughter, Lauren, had also met an amazing young man through the ministry of the Ramp. His name was Samuel Bentley. They were married on August 4, 2006.

For several years, all my children worked in various roles at the Ramp as we built that ministry together. As for me, in many ways it was like living a dream. I was sharing a God-given mission with my daughters and their husbands. Samuel was serving as CFO of the Ramp, and Lauren was teaching in the school of ministry and directing our conferences. Casey and Lindsey were serving as pastors of Ramp Church. Casey was directing the Ramp School of Ministry and Lindsey overseeing the performing arts department of the school and choreographing dances for Chosen. Each of them in their own way had contributed to the very DNA of the Ramp.

The first few years of Casey and Lindsey's marriage seemed wonderful. Within the next five years, they were blessed with two beautiful little girls, Analeise and Katie. Lindsey loved being a wife and mother. She was an excellent cook and enjoyed preparing meals for their family and decorating the house according to the upcoming season. Never did I foresee the storm that was about to hit our houses and the ministry.

A Cloud Forms

Spring is beautiful in Northwest Alabama. The earth is rebounding from the grips of winter, and everything is coming alive. The flowers are blooming, the birds singing and nesting, the woodland critters moving about, and the hills brimming with every imaginable shade of green! But in these parts of Alabama, spring has a sinister side; it's notorious for tornadoes.

Spring storms are something to behold. The lightning streaks across the sky while the bass thunder shivers a house, rattling windows and all else in it. I will admit, when I was a child, there was something kind of enjoyable in a good spring storm, however.

Grandmother would gather up Janet and me and head to the storm house. Now, there was nothing like the excitement of running in the rain with Grandmother and Grandpa from the front porch to the underground storm cellar Grandpa had built right beside the house. He had fashioned a door on top of it made out of a halved metal barrel with handles welded onto it so that you could lift it—if you were strong enough, that is. Once it was lifted, we quickly walked straight down the concrete steps that led into the small underground room. Sitting against the concrete wall, there was a wooden bench just big enough to hold about six people. It faced the wooden shelves that Grandmother used every year to store all her canned apples and tomatoes from her summer garden. The air smelled like the musty earth mixed with the smoky kerosene from the lantern Grandpa held to give us our only light. I was always a little concerned about the spiders, crickets, and other varmints we shared the space with, but Grandpa would take care of them, if need be. Of that, I was sure.

Once the thunder subsided, we knew it was safe to leave the cellar. I can still remember how Grandpa looked as he would slowly lift the heavy metal door and peer outside. Before he'd ever let us out, he always looked to make sure everything was still there. And it always was, at least until 2011.

The spring of that year had a rather peculiar start. In March, a local pastor in Hamilton contacted me with a rather strange message. A prophet named Joe Brock, whom I didn't know at the time, began to prophesy in a meeting that was held in Birmingham, Alabama. Strangely, he prophesied during his actual message, saying that an F5 tornado was heading toward Hamilton—Hamilton, Alabama!

Furthermore, he explained the reason it was heading our way was because of a fortified army of youth that was there, an army called to be gatekeepers of the Southeastern Conference, something I thought was a reference to the regional football league. The prophet suggested someone get word to us so that we could begin to pray.

After I was told about the word, I thought it was possibly the warning of a spiritual storm—something the Ramp and our leadership would pray about. I figured we would storm Heaven to stop the predicted storm, and then all would be well. And that's what we did. Little did I realize the warning prefigured both a literal physical cyclone and an actual spiritual tempest!

The Storm Strikes

About six weeks later, on April 27, 2011, the world changed for me and our community. The day began with warnings from our local meteorologist of an unusual weather pattern that could produce violent tornadoes. At 4:30 a.m., we were awakened by the sound of the warning sirens telling us a tornado was in the area. I got up, went to the front porch, looked around, and couldn't see anything. I didn't take the warning too seriously because, in these parts, warnings had become quite common. I did what any right-minded woman would do; I went back to bed.

When I woke up a little bit later, I prepared breakfast and turned on the news to listen to any weather updates. I discovered the storms throughout Alabama were intensifying. Although I was concerned, I went about my day as usual. I do remember walking outside to the porch and looking at the sky again.

My eyes scanned over the landscape of the countless trees lining the old dirt road that runs the length of our land. I saw the Millhouse. Before I was born, my grandfather had built it to house the old gristmill that overlooks the creek running beside our home. I had only begun to restore it in hopes it could be a place our family could gather for special events. I thought of the oak and pecan trees my grandfather had planted with the foresight of the property's and family's need for shade. I reflected on my family and the love we have had for the property. But I'm embarrassed to admit, in all my deliberation, I didn't once think of the prophetic warning. I just kept moving through that day's schedule.

By mid-afternoon, having recently returned home from shopping at the grocery store, I began to prepare lunch. I put together the quick fixings of spaghetti on the stove when I heard the local weatherman say, "We have just spotted a tornado in this area of Hamilton, Alabama."

I glanced quickly at the screen to see the forecaster pointing slightly north of Hamilton, right where I knew our house to be. Immediately, my phone started ringing. I answered it and hit speaker.

"Mom!" It was the very distressed voice of Lindsey. "Get over here to our basement now!"

Rick looked at me and said, "Let's get out of here!"

I turned the stove off and called my mother, "Mom, a tornado's coming. Rick and I are coming to get you and Dad right now. So, get Dad ready!"

Rick and I jumped into the Denali and drove across the street to pick up my parents. Some time back, my dad had suffered a stroke and was in need of daily assistance. He was having to move much more carefully and slowly than he used to, and he was no longer able to understand the urgency of such a moment.

Rick and Mom helped Dad get loaded in, and off we went. As we pulled out of their drive, the first tree went down right in front of us. Rick quickly swerved around it. But then another went down. He spun the steering wheel, maneuvering us by the tree.

At that point, Rick floored the vehicle and sped off, driving as fast and hard as he could to get us out of the valley. I noticed the standing trees were swirling or bending in the same direction. I knew we were in trouble. I was shaken and scared as I wondered what was happening to our home—to Grandmother's front porch and Grandpa's Millhouse.

Since Lindsey and Casey lived only about a mile away, we got right to their house and met them in the basement, where they had already taken shelter. Within a few minutes, we received a phone call.

"Hackleburg is gone," the voice on the phone said.

Hackleburg was a quaint little town about twelve miles north of the valley. My grandmother was raised there. It didn't seem possible that it could have been "gone."

We tried our best to keep calm, to help the children with their fears. It seemed like forever as we waited. But, thank God, things finally calmed down outside. It was evident the tornado had passed, and that was when Rick and Casey decided to go back to check on things at our property. There was so much debris in the road that Rick wanted me to stay behind with my parents and the kids.

About forty-five minutes later, they returned. As they walked into Lindsey's house, I noticed Casey had a hurt look on his face. He looked at us and said, "It's destroyed. The place is just destroyed."

Immediately, I thought of the beautiful pecan tree that stood right beside the house. My grandmother loved that tree. Its trunk was so huge it would have taken two people to get their arms around it. Its shade was enormous. I thought it was the prettiest tree in Hamilton.

"What about Grandmother's pecan tree?" I suddenly blurted out.

"It's lying on top of the house," Casey sadly replied.

I looked at Rick and said, "Take me to the valley."

We couldn't take the normal road. It was covered in trees. That meant we would have to return the back way, down Love Joy Road. The road surely didn't resemble either of those two emotions to me. I saw damage everywhere.

As we topped the hill to enter the valley, the view took my breath away. Over one hundred trees were lying all over the property—even some of Grandpa's trees! They had been full and majestic only an hour or so before. Now, they were lying on the ground.

The tall pines that covered the hill in the pasture were scattered like toothpicks. The few trees that remained were splintered and wounded.

Then there were the renovations we had finished only that week on the Millhouse. The new porch on it was gone. Grandpa's chicken house was gone. Grandmother's glider that matched her swing and had sat on the front porch all my life was found twisted in the tops of the fallen oaks. Pieces of the tin roof from Grandpa's barn were snaked into the trees tattering the ground with the storm debris that was everywhere.

With no umbrella, I got out of the SUV, walked around in the pouring rain, and sobbed. I was mourning over more than damaged new construction. I was weeping over the wreckage of the place that held my happiest memories—the place where I felt safe, loved, accepted, and free to be me. It was the first place— the foundational place—where my faith in God was built. Right above where those pine trees lay, as a child, I had heard the Voice in the wind calling me to preach.

It was all too much for me to take in. The tornado had happened so suddenly. All had been well, and within moments, a dark, evil enemy had swept across my land, wrenching and destroying its beauty. I simply could not see how it could ever be the same.

Grandmother's house—our house—was quite damaged by the large pecan tree. It now rested on top of the house, as Casey had said. But there was one thing that comforted me. Though all of the recent additions and renovations we had made to the property had been demolished, those things my Grandfather had built, all those years ago, had withstood the storm. That spoke to me. He had used strong, thick oak and spared no effort to build for the storm.

The trees that had fallen could be replanted, and with time the land would heal. But I found great consolation in knowing that what could have never been replaced—the things Grandfather's hands had built—had remained. It gave me hope.

The Aftermath

Rick and I had to move out for a few weeks as we began the extensive cleanup and repair. As the days turned to weeks, I began to realize how much there was to be thankful for. We were all alive. That was the miracle.

The series of tornadoes that mowed through the state of Alabama that day killed 243 people. The only F5 tornado to strike a destructive path through neighboring communities began its descent over our city of Hamilton. It took the lives of fifty precious people within a thirty-mile radius of my home. It was a ravaging reaper, a cruel twister.

When everything had calmed down, and we were rebuilding, I remembered the prophetic word given by Joe Brock. Sadly, Hamilton was hit by an F5 tornado, just as he said it would be. Only in retrospect did I realize the physical twister, after wielding its powerful devastation on life and property, exposed and foretold a spiritual disaster in the making.

That day marked the beginning of a storm in my personal life that would last almost five years. The storm itself seemed to be a sign of what was now upon us in a spiritual sense. It came quickly and unexpectedly. I had weathered other storms in my life, but I had never experienced anything like this one.

It was after this storm that I had noticed something had begun to change in Lindsey. There seemed to be a growing disinterest in the responsibilities of being a wife and mother. Even though I had placed her in the role of being the director of the performing arts department of the ministry, I would never have expected her to place that position before her home and family. And she knew that. Yet she seemed to be intentionally becoming obsessed with her job. It was as if she were making a conscious effort to see that her ministry was consuming her time.

I could sense the rising tension between her and Casey. I tried to talk with her about the unnecessary conditions she was placing on her schedule, but she always had an excuse as to why the extra time and work were needed.

While I was concerned about her job obsession, I was becoming more concerned about her heart's affections. I began to have unspeakable thoughts and questions stirring inside me. I pushed back at the idea. *Maybe I'm making too much out of this*, I reasoned within myself.

I was wrong. The storm was moving in on us again. It was about to spin Lindsey out on a journey, and so many of us with her. It was meant to destroy everything in its path—our family, our ministry, and the very foundations of my faith. Instead, it taught me the power of God that is manifested through intercessory prayer and faith in His Word.

In the journey it led me on, I became an eyewitness to the greatest miracle I have ever seen.

Father. Father. Help me.

How do I get through this?

So many questions. So many things on my mind.

How do I let her go? How do you let a child go? How?

I've been trying to save her from these waters.

Now, to release her?

Oh, Father. Help me trust You.

Trust that You can save her.

Trust that You will do what only You can do.

Oh, God. I need You. I need You.

Save Lindsey from every plan of the enemy against her.

Yesterday started well and ended in a battle of the mind.

I am desperate for You. Please come now to save us.

I know You are here.

—March 25, 2014

Chapter Three

. . . . .

THE JOURNEY BEGINS

Over the next few years, our community went about rebuilding their homes, their businesses, and their lives. I guess you could say *change* was the operative word.

There were changes in the landscape of Hamilton and neighboring cities and towns.

There were changes at the Ramp from a season of transition the ministry had experienced.

And there were even changes in Lindsey, and not for the better.

By the time I realized Lindsey was different, it was too late. She had already been deeply infected by a deception that was changing her from the inside out. The charming, loving, carefree girl I had known was now a bitter, stoic, hard young lady who seemed to be hiding a very dark secret.

She seemed to be developing an unusually close relationship with a young man and some of the young singles in the Ramp Church community. I saw that she appeared to be spending more time with them than she spent with her husband and children at home. Most of her friends were involved with the dance ministry of the church.

Furthermore, rehearsal times for the dance ministry were now consuming most of Lindsey's days, and evenings. Even her clothes and hairstyle began to take on the look of her single friends rather than the classy, modest style she had previously sported. I noticed that she looked for any opportunity to have an excuse to be with one particular male friend and other single friends. When she was with them, she was light and carefree, always appearing to be amused by their company. But when she was with her family, she seemed dejected, distant, and obsessed with her cell phone.

It was obvious she was pulling away from her sister and me, and the closeness we had always shared. But most importantly, she was making it abundantly clear that she was putting distance between herself and Casey.

As the months passed, I could tell things were getting worse instead of better. Casey knew something was terribly wrong, but nothing about this was making any sense to him. I could see the heaviness and concern of it weighing down on him. He began to reach out to me, not only as a mother-in-law but also as a spiritual leader since he was pastoring the church my husband and I oversaw.

As the situation began to escalate, I suggested Casey and Lindsey go to marriage counseling. At this point, Casey was willing to try anything. However, every attempt that was made at counseling was met with an uncaring disinterest when it came to Lindsey's participation. She ignored the follow-up work and took on an attitude that was unnecessarily critical, where she implied the relationship was helpless.

Lindsey was purposefully finding every opportunity to make me more and more aware of her unhappiness in their marriage. I continued to reach out to her and offer her loving counsel, but each time I did it seemed like I hit an unmovable wall. It was as though she had already reached an inner resolve. As I would soon find out, she did not want a solution. She wanted out.

Her Final Answer

In March of 2014, Lindsey informed me she was on her way to my house. I anticipated her arrival with prayer. I wanted to pour out my heart to her as her mother. I also wanted to understand what was going on and why she was making decisions that would destroy her family. After all, she knew firsthand the pain she was causing her own children. She had experienced it herself when our home was broken.

Internally, I hoped, *Surely, this will be the moment that whatever is blinding her from the truth will be shattered. She will listen to me. We've had many of these talks through the years as she worked her way through the challenges of teen relationships and personal identity. It will be like other times where she realizes what's wrong and how she needs to meet with God and let Him change her heart.*

When Lindsey arrived, we sat down together at my kitchen table. I began to talk to her as a mother talks to a daughter. I said, "Lindsey, there are two paths in front of you. Both of them have their challenges."

I could see the look on her face. She was obstinate. She wasn't interested in what I was about to say, but I continued anyway, "One path will require you work hard at repairing your marriage. But Casey loves you, and he is willing to do whatever it takes to heal your heart and your home."

I paused momentarily, looking for some kind of clue in the expression on her face. No, she didn't seem open to that option, I gathered, so I persisted with my words.

"The other path is alluring, Lindsey, because it is calling you to a perceived freedom. This voice is trying to convince you that you are in a prison in this marriage. It is lying to you and saying that you are being controlled and kept from fulfilling all the dreams that are in your heart. But the truth is, the only place of true freedom is found in being in the perfect will of God! Marriage is the will of God. It is not God's desire for your marriage to be destroyed and the lives of your children to be torn apart so that you can fulfill a dream you think God has put in your heart!

"Lindsey, we know the priorities of our lives. First, our personal relationship with God. Second, our marriage and family. Third, our ministry to others. Ministry cannot come before our families. There is no way God would ask you to break your covenant to Casey to fulfill a dream of your own. This is a plan of the enemy to destroy your life. He is telling you that you are in a prison in your marriage, and you are a 'bird' that needs to fly to your freedom, when in truth, you are living in freedom now, and the voice you are listening to is luring you into a deep, dark prison you've never known. Please, Lindsey, don't take this path. It will destroy your life. *I'm begging you to listen to me!*"

Uncomfortable and anxious, she sat in the chair, arms folded, eyes dark. Finally, she spoke, "You cannot tell me God's will for my life. No one can tell me that!"

"But, Lindsey, God's will for our lives has already been laid out for us in His Word. I'm only telling you what He has already made clear for us!"

For an hour and a half, I poured out my heart and my love with everything in me and every way I knew how. There were moments I thought she was possibly hearing me—moments I thought I could see the slightest movement of her heart toward the truth that was so evident. Now, it was time for the conversation to be over. I'd try one more time to bring her back to the truth and back to her family.

Everything in me was hoping and praying this would be the instant she'd come to her senses and have a change of heart.

With everything hinging on her answer, I asked, "So, Lindsey, after all that has been said, what is your final answer?"

"It's over. I want a divorce."

Pain shot through my body. *She didn't just say that. She couldn't have said that.* Trouble, I was prepared for. Counseling, I was prepared for. Even separation, I could have swallowed hard and accepted that, with the expectation she would get over this phase she was in and return to Casey. But divorce?! That blew me away!

As a mother, I knew this decision would cost her everything. My heart ached for her, for Casey, and for their two precious little girls who would have to walk this path. They all would have to take the journey with her. And she'd be bringing the rest of us with her, too.

Though my whole being was in pain, like someone took a baseball bat and struck my stomach, by the grace of God, I managed to respond to her as calmly as I could.

"It hurts me so deeply to know this is your final decision," I said, trying to hold myself together. "I love you, Lindsey. I will be here for you as much as I can, but I cannot stand with you in agreement for something that I know will destroy your life."

With that, Lindsey stood up, picked up her keys off the kitchen table, and walked out the door, leaving me in the deepest pain I'd ever known.

His Final Answer

I knew where I had to go. For me, this path is well worn. It always leads me to my place of safety—my place of healing, hope, and peace. It's the path to His Presence.

That night, I didn't drag myself outside to the front porch swing, though that surely would have offered me some comfort. Instead, I chose the Ramp, a place so precious to my heart and a place of His Presence.

I walked into the empty sanctuary that for years had held the loud shouts and praises of the young people I had delighted in bringing before Him. Not long before, it had held the shouts of my daughter. I walked to the altar and fell on my face. With groans that cannot be uttered and with the cry of a mother in travail, I lifted my voice and emptied my heart to Him. I determined I didn't care how long it would take—I had to reach God.

Several hours passed. Then something happened.

As I was praying aloud, I heard His Voice. It was clear and distinct, resonating in my mind and spirit. He said, *"You asked for her final answer. You didn't ask for Mine."*

Instantly, I stopped praying. The Voice was so undeniable that I had nothing else to say. Now on my knees, I remained in silence for a few moments, breathless with wonder that He had even spoken to me and very curious to know what His "final answer" would be. Quite awestruck, though, I didn't ask the Voice for His answer. I was dumbfounded and had nothing left in me to carry on any more conversation.

Exhausted, and finally realizing it, I gathered my things and drove home. Since it was well past midnight, I wasn't able to share what had happened with anyone, but I couldn't just go to bed after such an encounter, so I sat down on the couch in my living room and stared off in the darkness.

The silence and shadow of the night enveloped me. I felt held by them both, as if they kept me in a safe place where I could begin to process my conversation with Lindsey and the words the Voice had said to me. My body finally persuaded me to try to rest.

Vzzzzzt! Vzzzzzt! I came awake to what I thought was an alarm but soon realized it was my cell phone vibrating. Looking at the screen, I saw the time was 7:00 a.m., and I read Lauren's name.

That's strange. She doesn't usually call me this early, I thought, almost missing her call. Swiping my cell's screen, I answered, "Hello?"

"Mom!" She didn't even stop to hear me respond. "I was up very early this morning praying for Lindsey. I was kneeling in front of a small bookcase in my bedroom when my eyes fell on a book written by Reinhard Bonnke. I felt to take it out and just open it, and when I did, these were the first words my eyes fell on, 'And *His answer* was *marriage.* Period.' Isn't that awesome, Mom?! God said His answer for Lindsey and Casey is marriage!"

You could have knocked me over. Only a few hours before, the Voice had said to me, "You asked for her final answer. You didn't ask for Mine." Now, He was giving me *His* final answer. And His answer *was* marriage. *Period.*

Lauren had no idea what she was actually saying to me. She didn't know what God had said to me the night before. I was so amazed I could hardly respond. Then, as if that were not enough of a miracle, she added, "And, Mom, out of over 600 pages in this book, that statement is on page 111."

The Promise

Page 111, I couldn't believe it! Only a few days before, the number had become significant to me, Lauren, and the Ramp.

The outbreak of tornadoes a few years back not only forecasted the spiritual storm that spun Lindsey out, but it also foretold of a storm that would hit our ministry.

The Ramp had been facing a financial crisis. Some changes had been made that resulted in a reduction of support. The pressure on the leadership was great. And upon me, personally, it was almost unbearable. On the one hand, there was my baby girl in one of the darkest nights of her soul, and on the other, the ministry God had birthed through me and my family was in one of its greatest struggles. All I really wanted to do was be alone with God and pray. But life and ministry required me to keep pressing on. And so I did.

One Sunday morning in March, while on the road, I ministered at Dwelling Place Church in Cleveland, Tennessee, with my friend, Judy Jacobs. Toward the end of the service, someone whom I did not know, handed me an envelope. I, in turn, handed the envelope to my assistant, Jessica, because we weren't at a time in the service where I could really open it or speak to the person who gave it to me. I entirely forgot about the envelope until the following day.

Back in Hamilton on Monday, I went over to the Ramp per usual, walked into the green room, and started talking with my son-in-law Samuel. Soon, Jessica walked in and said to me, "Here's the envelope someone gave you yesterday."

I took it from her hand and noticed there was no name or address, just this handwritten Scripture reference on the front, "Deuteronomy 1:11." I proceeded to open the envelope, noticing there was no letter or note inside, and thought that was unusual. What I did find inside was $111.00 in cash!

I said to Samuel, "Look at this." I showed him the envelope with its message and contents.

"That is so strange!" Samuel said, looking very perplexed. "Yesterday, during the Sunday morning service here at the Ramp, someone walked up to our Lauren and handed her a check for $111.00. You won't believe this, but in the bottom left corner of the check, they had written Deuteronomy 1:11!"

"Dear, Lord! Someone go and look up Deuteronomy 1:11 right now!" I exclaimed.

Quickly, one of us found a Bible and opened it to these words: "And may the Lord, the God of your ancestors, multiply you a thousand times greater and bless you as He promised!"

Faith surged through my heart that day! I knew the two gifts with the same Bible verse were no coincidence. For Lauren and me to receive—on the same morning between 10:00 a.m. and 12:00 p.m., while in two different *states*—an offering of $111.00 with the Deuteronomy 1:11 reference was a God thing. It had His name written all over it!

From that day forward, we began to see the number *111* in the most random places. It would be the license plate number on the car in front of me, the number I was given when I ordered food, or the room number of my hotel room when I traveled. It began to be so bizarre. Everyone around my family and me knew something supernatural was happening.

From the beginning, I knew God was telling us He was going to bless and increase the ministry a thousand-fold. The finances were going to come in, and we started to see that in the coming months.

But the day Lauren woke me up with the news that God's answer for Casey and Lindsey was marriage, I understood that the blessing from God would include His restoring their marriage.

How directly He had answered, how clearly He had spoken, and how specifically He had confirmed His word by His Word!

Perhaps what I loved the most, though, in His final answer was that He used the word *period* after the statement. It spoke of finality. With that simple word, He said, "That's it. That's My answer. Marriage. I'm not changing My mind. Final answer."

When God speaks, what He says is all that matters. Often, God will declare His plan and His will in the *beginning* of a situation.

As for me, I knew God had spoken. I had God's word on it. I knew what God wanted. He wanted Casey and Lindsey's marriage. Of course, I knew this by the written Word of God, but His spoken *rhema* word generated faith in me.

Romans 10:17 says, "Faith comes by hearing and hearing by the word of God." I had heard a word! It was clearer to me than ever. I decided to agree with God, knowing He agreed with me for their marriage. When two agree on a matter, it will be done. I knew I had all of Heaven's armies backing me up! Casey and Lindsey's marriage was the will of God. And that settled it—*111*!

Expecting the miracle any day, I wrote my word down on an index card, kept it in my Bible, and began to declare it, "And His answer was marriage. Period."

What I didn't realize was how long it was going to take before I received the fulfillment of His promise.

God hears. God answers. God is everything.

I have spent about four hours praying for Lindsey.

I know He has heard me.

I have such peace. Oh, such peace.

I am at rest in hope. Yes, my soul rests in hope.

I'm not to speak of or look at anything in the natural.

All of these circumstances will come to nought.

Only what is unseen is eternal.

What is unseen? His Word!

I will live on His Word.

His Word IS my final answer.

His Word is HIS final answer.

And HIS answer is marriage. Period.

—April 19, 2014

Chapter Four

.....

THE WAY FORWARD

After the talk with Lindsey, I didn't expect her to take immediate action. I can't explain why I didn't, other than I suppose a mother wants to hope beyond hope that something was going to be done or said that would open her eyes, causing her to see the truth and return Lindsey—the Lindsey that we knew—back to all of us.

Although I knew she was upset, wanted out, and wasn't interested in trying to resolve things with Casey, I didn't think she would up and leave soon thereafter. She did, though, leaving her family behind her and agreeing to share custody of the girls with Casey fifty percent of the time.

Yet, again, her choices and behavior shocked me. Seriously, there were times I wondered who in the world had taken my baby girl, because the girl inside my daughter's body was a complete stranger to me, to Lauren, to Casey, to all of us!

Less than a month later, on April 3, 2014, I heard a vehicle coming up my driveway. I looked through my living room window, beyond the shade of my front porch, and saw Casey's Jeep pulling up. He didn't get out immediately. Instead, he sat there leaning over the steering wheel, weeping.

I stood there watching him from my window. Even though I knew what the Lord had spoken to Lauren and me, the fallout from Lindsey's actions was heart-hurting and gut-wrenching sorrow. There was no way to escape it, as there was the visible proof sitting in the Jeep parked in front of my house. Usually resolute and strong, my son-in-law was now bent over his steering wheel, broken.

There were no words to describe the pain of this moment. Emotionally, it was all doing me in. *How can this be real? Casey is a man of God who loves his wife and children more than anything! Why is she doing this to him? This makes no sense.* I was bombarded by these thoughts and many more.

Finally, his Jeep door opened, and he began to walk toward my front door with his grief written all over his face. I opened my door as he slowly crossed the porch. He walked into my living room and sat down on the recliner. With tears coming down his cheeks, he said, "She is filing for a divorce today."

God, please, no. How can this be real? I had so hoped and prayed and begged that it wouldn't come to this.

He continued, "Why? Why?! Why would she do this? I don't want the girls to have to go through this."

What could I say to him? There was no rational reason for her behavior. I couldn't understand it myself. I couldn't excuse it. I loved my daughter and wanted God's best for her, and I knew this couldn't be that.

"I'm so sorry, Casey." That was the best I could do. "I'm so sorry."

We sat there and cried in a room filled with more questions than answers. Our world had been turned upside down. We were in shock and were like victims after a catastrophic event who roam around trying to get their bearings. All we had in that moment was our tears, and way down deep inside, we still had our faith.

The Immediate Fallout

After Lindsey filed for divorce, the situation surrounding not only our family but also the ministry began to escalate. After all, Casey was the pastor of Ramp Church and the director of the Ramp School of Ministry. No one just separates and files for divorce without there being a cause. But what was the cause? That's what everyone was wanting to know—even those who wanted to know for the wrong reasons.

What made things even worse was my daughter began accusing her husband of being abusive and controlling. I knew there was no truth to what she was saying. It was her way of getting out of the marriage, but to lie about it? To spread gossip that would ruin the reputation of the man she once loved? I couldn't wrap my head around it.

And then there were the things she said about me and the ministry. Here, too, she created a complete picture about us all that would make it easier for her to justify her actions. I knew there was a war raging inside her. When I would read or hear the things she was saying about us, the truth in my heart overrode the pain. I knew that she did not really believe these things. She was trying to hide something. And at the time, only God and Lindsey knew what that was.

Among the many concerns I had regarding the welfare of my daughter, her children, and my son-in-law, I struggled with what to say to the church, ministry students, and the many others around the world who had supported or had been somehow impacted by the ministry. How could I explain something I didn't understand myself, especially with the accusations and rumors that circulated as a result of the situation?

I knew the accusations were not true, but as a leader and mother, it was impossible to make a public statement explaining to the church all the details of the truth. The challenge I faced was how to find a way to protect and defend Casey against the onslaught of lies and allegations that were whirling around him while, at the same time, leaving a path for Lindsey to find her way home when she faced the truth.

The Ramp's board of directors were called in to meet with Lindsey and Casey. I knew the directors to be incredible men and women of God who loved both of them. I knew the directors would use discretion and wisdom in their handling the situation. We felt it best for Casey and Lindsey to each meet separately with the board. I, then, would meet alone with the directors to receive their counsel and hear their decision.

After Casey's meeting, the directors shared with me the brokenness of his spirit and his willingness to do whatever it took to save his marriage.

I was thankful that Lindsey was willing to meet with the directors at all and hoped with all my heart that this might be a turning point. She walked into a room with people who had known her for years. She knew they loved her. My heart was burning with the hope that they could speak a truth into her that would shatter the deception.

During the entire time they met, I was alone in my house calling on God with everything I had in me. In my mind, I kept envisioning her walking out of the room with tears rolling down her cheeks, broken and free.

Sadly, it wasn't to be. After the meeting, she stormed into my house, more calloused and angrier than ever, picked up her keys, and took off down my driveway in her car.

With an anxious heart, it was now my turn to meet with the board to hear the result of their conversations. With everything in me, I was hoping that maybe something had been said to her that had broken through. Or maybe they had somehow seen a glimmer of hope in her. That wasn't the case. Instead, they each had a similar look on their faces that said it all. One of them broke the horrible silence by simply saying, "I'm so sorry, Karen."

I had to walk directly from the board meeting into the Ramp. A special meeting had been called to share with the church and school what was going on. The auditorium was packed with people who were confused and concerned by the rumors that were now rampant.

I trembled as I walked onto the platform to face the Ramp Church and the ministry students that night. Though the board of directors were so gracious and affirming to me, I knew I'd have to say something at some point. I remember thinking, *How is this happening? Is this real, or am I having a nightmare? God, if this is a nightmare, please let me wake up!* I didn't wake up. I felt that sick feeling—that awful feeling of grief. It's almost otherworldly. Although I was deeply concerned for our Ramp Church family and our precious students, my heart was aching for Casey and longing for Lindsey.

With much love and concern, the board made the announcement that Lindsey had filed for divorce. They clearly stated that, after meeting with both of them, there were no biblical grounds for the divorce. They explained that, after meeting with Casey, they did not feel it was right or necessary to remove him from his current position as pastor of the church, but they were recommending he take a three-month sabbatical of prayer and rest as he was working through the situation at hand.

Then it was my turn to say something. Trying to conceal the fear that was in my heart, I took the podium to face the people who had laid down their lives to join with me in the Ramp's mission. I reminded them of the faith that had helped us to weather the storms of the past, assuring them we would get through this one as well and make it to the other side.

I opened my Bible and began to read words written by the apostle Paul. They seemed to best describe where we were as a family and what was needed most—prayer:

> *We think you ought to know, dear brothers and sisters, about the trouble we went through in the province of Asia. We were crushed and overwhelmed beyond our ability to endure, and we thought we would never live through it. In fact, we expected to die. But as a result, we stopped relying on ourselves and learned to rely only on God, who raises the dead. And he did rescue us from mortal danger, and he will rescue us again. We have placed our confidence in him, and he will continue to rescue us. And you are helping us by praying for us.*
> *—2 Corinthians 1:8–11*

As the leader of the ministry, I felt the responsibility to steady the ship somehow. As Lindsey's mom, everything in me wanted to run out of the building to find her. I hated the thought that she was hurting, that we were talking about her life without her being present. It felt like a death had occurred.

I hated even more knowing the pain she was experiencing was coming from the choices of her own making. Mothers are supposed to be with their daughters when they are in pain to bring comfort and love. *To comfort her in this pain, however, would be to sympathize with a lie that she was believing.*

It was here, in this very hard place, that I experienced how real love is expressed. When you truly love someone, you will never "agree with" or support any decision they are making that you know will ultimately destroy them. *Real love is always expressed in real truth.*

Jesus loves every man and woman the same. He doesn't play favorites. Yet, in His dealings with the Pharisees, He seemed almost harsh and offensive. In reality, His love for them was expressed in His words of truth that cut them to the core.

The spirit of religion was destroying them, and the only way they could be free was to hear the truth of their condition, even if it made them hate Him, reject Him, and ultimately kill Him. This kind of love comes at a great price.

It is a selfish, soulish love that comforts people in their deception. Deep within dwells a hidden motive that sometimes only God knows. The end result of this kind of relationship is deadly for the "comforter" as well as for the deceived.

After the dreaded announcement, it was unbelievably hard for me to watch people surround Lindsey with their counsel and comfort, knowing they did not know the whole truth of the situation. Neither were they in a position to know that truth. Their attempts at helping and comforting her were actually causing more harm to her than good. It was a painful experience for me to watch.

Perhaps one of the greatest tragedies in all of this was that many of her comforters ended up being casualties of the conflict happening inside her. Relationships were broken, and friendships were lost. Deception and offense have a way of changing people. Many never recover.

That night, I wrote in my journal:

Unspeakable things happened today.

I am pressing into my Father.

This is too big for me.

Have handed it all over to God, the best way I know how.

I've been asking God to throw this enemy into confusion for me. Yes! All of these enemies involved in this demonic conspiracy against me and my family, throw them into utter confusion!

Then I ask, "How do You do that, Lord?"

He spoke to me. He said the way to put the enemy into con-fusion is to love. Satan expects us to fight with anger, violence, retaliation, gossip, and hate. But the best way to confuse him is to love. He doesn't know what to do with love. That's why the cross "confused" the enemy.

The cross left the world asking the question, "What kind of love is this?"

Oh, God, help me to love these people that have hurt me so much. Yes, even those who consider themselves my enemies.

Heaven's Answer

It was April 11, 2014, early in the morning. Much had transpired since Casey came to see me and Ramp Church had been informed of Lindsey's filing for divorce. I was at home, sitting on the couch overwhelmed with fear and deep turmoil.

How can this be happening? How can a girl raised in the Presence of God be so far away from everything she has ever known to be right? I struggled to understand. Desperate for a word from God, I was searching through my Bible and praying, "God, speak to me! Tell me something!"

Ding. I recognized the sound. Someone had sent me a text. I picked up my phone and looked down to see it was a message from one of my spiritual sons, Joe Reeser, whom I knew had been pray-ing for me. He sent me two verses from Isaiah 49:24–25.

I read the text aloud: "Who can snatch the plunder of war from the hands of a warrior? Who can demand that a tyrant let his captives go? *But the Lord says,* 'The captive of the warrior *will be released*, and the plunder of the tyrant *will be retrieved*. For I will fight those who fight you and *I will save your children.*'"

I was as a dead woman coming to life—a spineless rag doll suddenly standing straight and tall.

As I read the words, they spoke like a voice declaring a confident command. I knew I had heard from God. Once again, He spoke to me just when I needed it. A wave of peace swept over me that lasted all of about five hours.

That evening, I was scheduled to speak for a women's conference in Jackson, Mississippi. While I was traveling in the car to the event in the afternoon, I received a phone call informing me that Lindsey was on her way to stay with her father and his wife in another state. Lindsey had not had a close relationship with her father from the time of our divorce. Since her decision to leave her husband and the ministry, they had developed a new relationship. He was endeavoring to support her during what he perceived to be a very difficult time. This would have been a wonderful thing had he understood the truth of the matter.

As we traveled south on a bumpy interstate, I sat quietly, staring out the backseat window. It was as though I could see straight through the blue sky and into the fiery eyes of my Father God. Since there were other people in the car, I couldn't pray like I really wanted to, but I knew He could see into my heart and hear my desperate cry.

Please, God, please help me. Take away this fear. Please speak to me again.

Ding. There went my phone again. It was another text. I looked down to see a message from a wonderful young woman of God, Mandy Adair. The text read, "Felt to send you this passage from Isaiah 49:24–25, 'Who can snatch the plunder of war from the hands of a warrior? Who can demand that a tyrant let his captives go? But the Lord says, the captives of warriors will be released, and the plunder of tyrants will be retrieved. For I will fight those who fight you, and I will save your children.'"

I was almost breathless. It was the exact same scripture I had received only a few hours earlier. The same word *twice* in the same day!

In this moment of fear and struggle, my Father was reminding me of His promise. It was Heaven's answer that I clung to like a drowning man taking hold of a life preserver in a storm-tossed sea. Once I was back on dry ground, the words of this promise became a sword in my hand. I swung it often, declaring the power of its reality over and over.

The Fight

On one particular day, I was in the Millhouse praying when something unusual happened. I began to see it.

Clearly, like a vision of the soul, I could see a long, rectangular, windowless, concrete building with one door on the end as an entrance. Sitting in a chair, beside the door, was a large creature, somewhat similar in appearance to the Orcs from the movie *The Lord of the Rings*. This demonic being was there to guard the entrance of the building. I knew this was a place of bondage, a prison, similar to a hellish concentration camp. Lindsey was being held captive inside this horrible place. It was as though I could see her sitting in a small room, chained to a chair. She appeared almost lifeless in the despair of deception.

Many, many times, as I prayed, I would physically walk forward in a "spiritual" virtual reality of sorts and wield the weapon of the Word that my Father had given me. I would mentally focus on that demonic being guarding Lindsey's prison door and boldly say, "Who can snatch the plunder of war from the hands of a warrior? Who can demand that a tyrant let his captives go? *The Lord says*, the captives of the warrior—Lindsey—*will* be released and the plunder of tyrants—her marriage, home, finances—*will* be retrieved! For God says, I will fight those who fight you, and I will save your children!"

After speaking these words, I would physically turn around and walk off. Day after day, I approached this place, this enemy, with the weapon of the Word.

One day, to my unexpected amazement, as I was declaring the taunting word of the Lord, I went into another vision. I saw the door open, and I saw Lindsey begin to walk out! She was simply walking forward, staring straight ahead. I was so stunned I could hardly believe what I was seeing!

Then, before I had time to even take in what I was experiencing, I looked and following Lindsey out the prison door was an endless stream of young men and women walking into their freedom. Some of them were dancing, others were singing, some appeared to be playing invisible musical instruments, and others were acting as though they were in a theater. There were so many coming out that I could not see the end of the multitude. I wept realizing that the battle I was in for my daughter was not only for her, but for all those who would be delivered through her testimony!

This experience helped me to understand why the warfare was so fierce. It wasn't just Lindsey's deliverance at stake. This fight was for the deliverance of a multitude of other sons and daughters also being held captive by the power of this demonic influence. It gave me new strength and determination to hold my ground, declaring the authority that is found in the Word of God. I didn't know when, but I knew that someday the door of this dreadful place was going to open and Lindsey was coming out. But she was not coming out alone!

Walking in prayer, from one end of the Millhouse to the other, I declared it loudly, with everything I had in me, "*All of these captives will be released!*"

My body is here. My mind is there.

Praying constantly it seems.

Looking. Waiting on God. Hoping. Longing.

Fighting the good fight of faith. Rebuking fear.

Oh, God, help me believe. Help me to trust You.

I am believing His Word over ANYTHING I see or hear.

Sometimes I find myself full of faith and assured of hope.

Other times I find myself screaming in fear and despair.

Oh, how weak I feel sometimes.

Oh, how this has revealed the smallness of my faith.

But I press on. Hoping in my God.

—May 23, 2014

Chapter Five

.....

STANDING—UNTIL

How do you describe the love a mother feels for her child? It's a love that doesn't diminish or decrease as the child ages.

How do you just turn off the passionate protective nature you experience when you see your child heading toward a danger that you know will take her life? You can't, at least I couldn't.

How does a mother turn and walk away from a child drowning in an ocean of deception? She doesn't. She jumps in and tries to pull her daughter to shore—even if it means hurting her child in the process!

It is painful to be misunderstood, especially when your most sincere intentions to help are turned to accusations of being a "controlling mother."

I remember a particular conversation with a professional Christian counselor I contacted as I wanted to gain insight and receive help as a mother who was walking through this mess. I called him on my cell phone. I gave him the gist of what had been going on in Lindsey's life and how I was trying to handle it. In a voice and tone that felt so uncaring, he sternly stated, "You've *got* to get *out* of this!"

The words hit painfully hard. Logically, what I was told made sense and seemed like the right thing to do. Walk away, and let it go. Get out of it, and go on with my life. After all, she was an adult and would make her own decisions.

I can see how it is easy to give advice when you are not the one feeling the pain of seeing your child's life being torn apart by an unseen enemy. There was only one problem with this counsel. I simply couldn't seem to find the "get out of this" button inside my heart. Oh, believe me, there were many days the pain was so deep, especially when I was learning of Lindsey's continued dark descent, I would have pressed a button, any button, if I had it and knew it would give me some relief! But the truth is, after talking to so many mothers in this world, I could have told the counselor that button doesn't exist for many of us.

I also found, if you allow yourself to listen to the accusations of the enemy, you will find yourself in a no-win situation. He will work hard to make you feel like, in some weird way, it *was* all your fault. It was hard to deal with statements like "You've always been too involved in your kids' lives," "You spoiled your kids when they were young," or "You were overprotective."

There were other times when I was "counseled" through the recounted stories of other people in similar "hopeless" situations. These, I was assured, had learned how to cope and just move on with their lives.

I understood people meant well. They were coming from a place of love and had good intentions, but basically they were telling me through their stories to accept Lindsey's decision and get on with my life.

"This is her decision," they would say. "You cannot control her decisions. After all, she's a grown woman. And you have a life to live. You can't let this destroy your life, too. You must accept this and move on."

Move on? Forgive me, but my mind was screaming, *How am I supposed to just move on? My son-in-law, whom I love like a son, is devastated, my two precious granddaughters are hurting and confused, and my daughter is about to walk off the edge of a cliff. And you want me to "move on"?!*

While my mind wrestled with these thoughts, my spirit was in full resistance. It grew louder than my thinking and shouted an unequivocal, "*No!*"

Then the Spirit reminded me what I was being told was not the will of God. Nothing about this looked like the Father. Nothing about this lined up with what His Word said or what His personal promises to me were. His desire was for marriage. Period. 111!

And, as if I could add anything more to that, I remembered "The captive of the warrior will be released."

Jesus said in John 10:10, "The thief's purpose is to steal and kill and destroy. My purpose is to give them a rich and satisfying life!"

The breakup of Casey and Lindsey's marriage was clearly the work of the thief and destroyer. It was not God's will that her life and marriage be destroyed. I determined in God not to sit down and allow the enemy to rob my family and wipe out their purpose. I refused to move on with my life if it meant surrendering to the enemy.

Really? Are we just at the will of the enemy of our souls to wreak havoc on our lives, and we have no ability to do anything about it? Heaven, no!

Though journeying at times through grief, I grew resolute. I was not going to sit this one out. I was not going to be sidelined by my sorrow, my pain, some else's counsel, or the adversary. My heart was fixed on continuing to hear the Voice tell me His word on this particular matter.

Then I would stand in faith, declaring *that word* over my daughter until my daughter looked like *that word!*

Lindsey had made her decision—divorce. God had made His decision—marriage. I made my decision: I'm standing—until!

The Power of Agreement

I quickly realized that, to fight this fight of faith, everything in my world would have to change. The fight would require an intense focus. The normal priorities of my schedule would have to give way to the priority of directed, persistent, intentional prayer. Fervently, I would need to seek the Lord.

The first thing I discovered was the intercessory burden was too much for me to bear alone. Throughout my life, my mother had taught me the power of agreement through these scriptures:

> *"Again I say to you that if two of you agree on earth concerning anything that they ask, it will be done for them by My Father in heaven."*
>
> —*Matthew 18:19*

> *"Take this most seriously: A yes on earth is yes in heaven: a no on earth is no in heaven. What you say to one another is eternal. I mean this. When two of you get together on anything at all on earth and make a prayer of it, my Father in heaven goes into action. And when two or three of you are together because of me, you can be sure that I'll be there."*
>
> —*Matthew 18:19–20 (MSG)*

Jesus said, "If two agree concerning anything they ask." These were not my words; they were Jesus' words. Oh, the unlimited expanse of this promise! He said, "Anything." When we ask for anything, according to His will, we can have what we are asking for.

The key word in the passage, of course, was the word *agree*. The power of this word was released in my life and the situation I was combatting when I had perfect agreement with someone else in prayer. I knew the Greek word for *agree* was *sumponeo*, which meant to be in agreement with, in unison or one accord. It meant to speak together with agreement—to be harmonious and united. Furthermore, it meant to agree with and declare the statements agreed upon, or regard something as settled, like a reached agreement.

I had preached on the power of agreement—how the power of God was released when we find someone who would stand with us and decree *only* what the Word of God said. That individual had to be unmoved by natural circumstances—someone who was in perfect harmony with us in prayer and had an ear to hear what the Spirit was saying.

I had to find those who were called to carry this burden with me—whose assignment it was to pray for Casey and Lindsey's marriage. There were many people who were praying for Lindsey during this time. I'm so very thankful for each one of them.

There were several who went beyond the call of duty to join me in prayer. Those who stood with me in strong agreement were members of my family and an intimate circle of friends. They kept watch. They persevered with me in faith.

There was one lady, though, who was a God-send in my life for the entirety of my journey of intercession. Her name was Pam Barnett.

For more than two years, Pam made herself available for prayer literally 24/7. We prayed in absolute agreement, believing that God was going to bring Lindsey home. Period. We wept together, shouted together, and decreed the Word of the Lord, at the top of our lungs, together. On the days when the battle was the most intense and I was struggling to keep believing, she would preach to me, "We are *not* giving up! We will not be moved! What God said is going to come to pass!"

When I couldn't pray or even speak, I would hold the phone to my ear while she quoted the promises God had given me.

Pam and I declared countless times, in the worst of times, "Casey Doss loves Lindsey Doss, and Lindsey Doss loves Casey Doss." This was the will of God, and we knew it. Every time we agreed upon and decreed these words into the opposing atmosphere, the power of God was released to bring it about. We understood that there was power in the Word and will of God, and that there was power in agreement!

Like Frodo and Samwise, from *The Lord of the Rings: The Return of the King*, we shared a burden. In the movie, Frodo's burden was too great for him to carry alone. The mission required both of them to give their all to focus on one thing—destroying the evil ring. When Frodo could go no further, Samwise gathered all his remaining strength and said, "I can't carry your burden, but I can carry you." With that being said, he picked up Frodo and carried him up the mountain to the place where the victory was ultimately won. Pam did the same for me. Forever, I will be truly grateful for her and the other godly people who stood with me.

The Power of Prayer

What do you do when you don't know what to do? You pray.

What do you do when you don't know what to pray? You rely on your Other precious prayer partner, the Holy Spirit.

As Deuteronomy 32:30 says, "One can put a thousand to flight, two can put ten thousand!" When I didn't have a thousand or one, for that matter, I reminded myself what my mother taught me.

She said, "When I don't have anyone around to agree with, I just say, 'Holy Ghost, I agree with You!'"

Jesus said,

> *And I will pray the Father, and He will give you another Helper, that He may abide with you forever—the Spirit of truth, whom the world cannot receive, because it neither sees Him nor knows Him: but you know Him, for He dwells with you and will be in you . . . But the Helper, the Holy Spirit, whom the Father will send in My name, He will teach you all things, and bring to your remembrance all things that I said to you.*
>
> *—John 14:16–17*

The Holy Spirit is the greatest prayer partner we could ever have. He *always* knows the will of the Father and is in perfect *agreement* with that will! Romans 8:26–27 reminded me on this journey that the Spirit is our Helper, and He is available at every moment of every day. He is *always* ready to pray with us and for us; in fact, He pleads for us in harmony with the Father's will. Essentially, when the Spirit prays for us, the Spirit is saying to the Father, "What You said, Father, so be it. Let it be done according to Your will." In other words, the Spirit is amen-ing the Father on.

Prayer is power! Holy Spirit-fueled prayer is nuclear power!

The Power of Fasting

Not only did the Holy Spirit help me pray, the Holy Spirit helped encourage and strengthen me through the testimonies of others.

Judy Jacobs is one of my dearest friends. She carries a powerful anointing as a minister of the Gospel. She and her husband, Jamie

Tuttle, pastor Dwelling Place Church. She is the director of the Women's Institute of Mentoring. Aside from being a great leader, Judy is a woman of prayer.

I knew the testimony of God's healing Judy's eldest daughter. Several years ago, the enemy attacked her daughter Kaylee. At the time, Kaylee was only eight years old. She had been admitted into the hospital in need of a true miracle. Judy set her face like flint in prayer. With an unrelenting resolve, she sought God for deliverance to come to her daughter. She began to fast. And as days and weeks began to pass, she continued to seek God with all her heart.

After some time, Jamie began to be concerned about Judy's physical condition. The intensity of the prayers and days with no food had begun to show. In loving concern, Jamie asked her, "How long are you going to do this?"

With grit and determination, Judy responded, "Until. Until! What's the devil going to do with *until*?!"

A few days later, Kaylee was out of the hospital, delivered by the power of God.

To be honest, I don't enjoy fasting. It has always been a challenge for me, especially in the beginning, but oh, the reward of it! I don't understand all about it, but I do know one thing: Fasting works!

For me, I noticed several things that happened when I prayed and fasted for Lindsey. It crushed my flesh and strengthened my spirit. When I fasted, I was more spiritually aware and sensitive to what was going on in the spirit realm. I heard God more clearly. It even increased my love for Him.

When I fasted, my flesh would whine and beg to be satisfied, but I often found my spirit conquering my flesh with these loud words, "I love God more than the food you are wanting. I want to hear from God more than I want to please you!"

Furthermore, denying my flesh food brought me into greater intimacy with God. He was moved by my fasting and would draw nearer to me. I felt the closeness of His Presence. And all this produced a confident rest inside my heart, enabling me to continue to stand—until.

I talked with her last night. Poured my heart out.

Went pretty rough.

After this conversation, I feel it is time to rest.

Rest in hope. Find rest in trusting.

Easier said than done.

But I'm trying.

Sometimes I feel strong and feel like I'm doing good.

Other times I feel weak and battle fear.

But . . . I will continue to stand.

Sometimes I feel strong in believing.

Other times I find myself asking, "Do I believe?"

But, Father, my final answer is, "Yes, I believe."

Words cannot express the emotions of my heart.

Waves of "overwhelmed" hit hard sometimes.

I just have to give it all to God. Too much. Too much.

Heaven and Earth would have to pass away if she were not saved out of this.

He cannot—He will not—fail His promise to me.

He is perfectly faithful.

—June 16, 2014

Chapter Six

.....

FAITH HOLDS ON

The date was November 22, 2014. I had heard more news about Lindsey and had come to another place of desperation, needing to hear something to give me hope.

My spirit had kept fighting the "good fight of faith," but the current circumstances landed some heavy blows. I needed others to tell me that they had been here before and had witnessed a miracle. Those I turned to knew too much about the situation.

In their experience, they had seen these scenarios played out all too often without the desired outcome. In their concern for me, they continued to encourage me to find a way to move on with my life. "This is her decision, and you have no control over it. You've got to let her go," they told me, their words only increasing the intensity of the battle within.

I do remember one conversation in particular. The individual was hoping I would find comfort in the fact that I had raised Lindsey in the Presence of God.

"When you train up a child in the way they should go, when they are old, they will not depart from it. Someday, Lindsey will come home. Even though her marriage will be lost, her children affected, her ministry gone, someday, she will come back to God," was the consolation I was given.

As soon as the words were spoken, I felt my heart sink to the pit of my stomach. This was not what I wanted or needed to hear. I just wanted to get out of the conversation as soon as I possibly could, go home, and get alone with God. I had some things to discuss with Him.

Losing Everything

I walked into my house and dropped my belongings down in a heap. Falling onto the floor of my living room, I began to call out to God from the depths of my soul. With my face turned toward the ceiling, I cried out, "Really, God? *Really*? Is this the way it's going to be? Someday, Lindsey will come home, but her marriage and ministry will be lost? Analeise and Katie will have to spend the rest of their lives torn between these two worlds of light and darkness?"

By this time, Lindsey and Casey were working out details for temporary custody arrangements. Though the divorce was not finalized, I was watching the events of her life continue to twist and gyrate further away from Casey and from God.

I continued my lament, "Really, God? Because that is *not* what I have asked You for! And that is *not* what You've been telling me. I asked You for Lindsey to return to You, to return to Casey, to return to her children, to return to her family, and to return to her ministry. *Answer me, God!* Tell me, now, if what this person has said is the truth, because I can't take the pain of believing in false hope—of being disappointed in the end!"

I walked to the front door and threw it open. Stepping onto my grandmother's porch—my porch—I said as loudly as I could, more or less screaming, "God! Satan has come into *my house* and taken *my daughter*, and *I want her back!*"

A righteous indignation exploded inside me! After the months of praying, watching, and looking for change in Lindsey, my heart wanted to get off the never-ending, no-fun, emotional roller coaster I was on. My head was spinning, and I wanted to see something, anything, to show me that all the believing, praying, standing, and fighting in faith was having some kind of effect.

Continuing to cry out in prayer, I heard something. It stopped my complaint. It was my Heavenly Father's familiar Voice.

"Declare this," He said. "'Today is the day of deliverance!'"

Like a little girl whose Daddy had told her to hush up and repeat after him, I began to say what Abba Daddy told me, "Today is the day of deliverance. Today is the *day* of deliverance. *Today* is the *day* of deliverance. *Today is the day of deliverance!*" I was finally getting the hang of it. The tenacity was coming back in me.

"Today is the day of deliverance! Today, November 22, 2014, is the day of deliverance! That's right! This day, November 22, 2014, is the day of deliverance!"

I shouted it over and over until I heard the Voice again. This time, He said, "Go to Prayer Mountain."

There is a dirt road that rambles up a hill on my property. On the side of the hill is a bluff, but it has always been a mountain to me. The Voice knew that's what I called the place.

I quickly gathered my jacket, my keys, and my Bible. I jumped on my buggy—it's actually a golf cart—and headed down the dirt road and up the hill to Prayer Mountain.

When I got to the top, I stepped off the buggy with my Bible in hand, and as I have done so many times before, I began to pace the top of the hill on my well-worn path. With my face heavenward, I was reminded why I loved this place so much. The blue sky was endless and seemed to open, revealing the power, majesty, and nearness of my Father.

I started praying and walking, walking toward the edge of the bluff that overlooks the dream I carry in my heart of what will someday be Camp Ramp. As I walked along the ancient rock, I happened to look down and noticed something on the rock beneath my feet. There were four words carved into the rock. I had never noticed them before, so I looked good and hard. In letters about two inches tall were these words, "The Place of Deliverance." My first thought was, *Today is the day of deliverance, and this is the place of deliverance!*

Almost breathless with wonder, I thought, *"What in the world? Where did that come from? I've never seen this before. Who. . . ,"* I was about to consider who had etched the words into the rock when the weightiness of God's Presence came over me.

As Moses experienced, I felt the ground I was standing on was holy. Immediately, I knelt, purposefully placing my knees on the letters. With my Bible buried in my chest, I cried out to Him again, "Answer me, God! Will it be as they have said? Will all be lost? Will her marriage be lost? Will her destiny and ministry be destroyed?"

I was exploding in awe and faith that the words were etched in the rock. I knew God had put them there for me. I didn't know who He used to carve them, but that didn't matter. God was speaking, and I wanted to hear what He had to say.

Between my questions and my tears of worship, I heard God speak again, "Go to Ziklag and to the Shunamite woman."

Recovering Everything

Even though I have often heard of these stories and read these passages in the past, at that moment, I couldn't remember the details of the stories. So, I opened my Bible, and there on my knees, I began to anxiously thumb through the pages, trying to remember the books and chapters they were found in.

Quickly, I found Ziklag in 1 Samuel 30:1–8. I began to read.

David and his mighty men had returned from the camp of the Philistines only to find their hometown of Ziklag raided and burned to the ground by the Amalekites. The Amalekites had taken captive the wives and children of David and his men. All seemed lost. In fact, David's mighty men were so distraught over the loss of their families that they talked about stoning David. Right then, David began to encourage himself in the Lord. That's when things began to shift:

> *Then he [David], said to Abiathar the priest, "Bring me the ephod!" So Abiathar brought it. Then David asked the Lord, "Should I chase after this band of raiders? Will I catch them?" And the Lord told him, "Yes. Go after them. You will surely recover everything that was taken from you."*
>
> *—1 Samuel 30:7–8*

There it was, right in front of my eyes! It was as if the Voice were speaking off the pages of the book I was holding in my hands. This was my answer from God! It was as though the very hills themselves were rumbling from the power of His Voice! I knew it was my answer. I was going to receive *everything* I had asked God for, and not just part of my request. Not only would Lindsey be returned to God, but she would be returned to Casey, her girls, her family, and her ministry! I wept. I shouted. I worshipped.

After I had calmed down a little, I remembered the Lord had told me to go to the Shunamite woman. I turned to see what He wanted to say to me about her. It was not the story I expected. I expected it to be the story of the time the Shunamite woman's son died.

In that story, she immediately found Elisha who came and raised her son from the dead. I loved that story, often finding encouragement in the resurrection of her son.

This time, my eyes fell on the portion of the story not often told:

> *Elisha had told the woman whose son he had brought back to life, "Take your family and move to some other place, for the Lord has called for a famine on Israel that will last for seven years." So the woman did as the man of God instructed. She took her family and settled in the land of the Philistines for seven years. After the famine ended she returned from the land of the Philistines, and she went to see the king about getting back her house and land. As she came in, the king was talking with Gehazi, the servant of the man of God. The king had just said, "Tell me some stories about the great things Elisha has done." And Gehazi was telling the king about the time Elisha had brought a boy back to life. At that very moment, the mother of the boy walked in to make her appeal to the king about her house and land. "Look, my lord the king!" Gehazi exclaimed. "Here is the woman now, and this is her son—the very one Elisha brought back to life!" "Is this true?" the king asked her. And she told him the story. So he directed one of his officials to see that everything she had lost was restored to her, including the value of any crops that had been invested during her absence.*
>
> *—2 Kings 8:1–6*

What about God?! *Everything* that she had lost was restored to her!

I heard God's answer to my questions. It was not going to be as "they" had said. It was going to be as "He" had said!

While I could release Lindsey and her family and her future to God, He was giving me so much Word to stir my faith to hold on to His promises and to her.

This was almost too much for me. I was overwhelmed. I shouted with all my might, *"Today, November 22, 2014, is the day of deliverance!"*

Somehow, I knew that was the day I had won the case.

Like David, my family too had been raided by the enemy. Like David, when I inquired of the Lord, He answered me, "I will surely recover all."

And like the Shunamite woman, I had taken my case to the court of Heaven. Appearing before the King and Judge, I had asked for the *full* restoration of all that had been taken from me. I stood in awe when the gavel struck His desk and the Judge of Heaven and Earth ruled in my favor.

I will surely recover all! And everything meant *everything!*

When I left Prayer Mountain that day—the place of deliverance—I was so stirred with faith, that I expected to get a phone call from Lindsey telling me she was coming home right then, on that day, November 22, 2014. That's how real the encounter had been.

However, the opposite happened. It got worse. Again.

I want to live in a place of trusting obedience.

A place of faith and patience.

What an interesting place that is!

The tension between faith and patience.

Faith feels like NOW!

Patience feels like wait.

Now! Wait. Now! Wait. Now! Wait.

Honestly, the pull between these two words is . . . exhausting.

Father, I want to please You.

I am asking You, deliver Lindsey today.

Save and heal their marriage.

Do it today, Lord.

Now! I wait on You.

—July 15, 2014

Chapter Seven

.....

HOPE RISES

Ephesians 6:12 says, "For we are not fighting against flesh-and-blood enemies, but against evil rulers and authorities of the unseen world, against mighty powers in this dark world, and against evil spirits in the heavenly places." These words gave perspective to my faith. I learned to never put a face on evil.

My war—your war—is not against people. My fight, in this case, wasn't really with Lindsey anymore. Neither was it against the people she had begun to hang out with or, more specifically, the young man whom she was seeing—the one who wasn't her husband.

She had been taken captive by a spirit of deception. Lindsey was living in a delusion. That I knew. The enemy had painted a picture for her of a world that didn't even exist. It was a "Neverland," where people didn't have to grow up and face adult responsibilities. She was so convinced of this fantasy that she was willing to forfeit everything that mattered to her in order to live a life in her imagined land.

Unwittingly, she believed the lies of the enemy that there was a place where she could experience "true freedom," a place where she could pursue her dreams. The adversary had duped her, but it didn't happened overnight. The enemy knew that wouldn't have worked on her.

Lindsey had been raised in the Presence. She herself had practiced the Presence. And she knew God's Word. There was no way an overnight takedown would have happened to her. Instead, the adversary worked slowly, over a period of a few years, to capture her. Thought by thought, conversation by conversation, her heart was led away. The enemy had managed to build a grid, a stronghold, in her mind. She filtered everything through it.

Whenever I had an opportunity, I tried to say something to bring her back around. It was as though she had become deaf to reason and truth. In fact, I found the more I tried to speak "truth" to her, the more resentful she became.

The conversations I had with her, then, wore me out. Anything I said was twisted or spun around. I thought I was losing my mind. Those conversations tended to make the situation worse, leaving me exhausted, hurt, and confused at times.

When I realized I couldn't reason with her, I understood I was dealing with the influence of a demonic spirit. Knowing this, I positioned myself in prayer. And when I prayed, I took the Word of God with me. I used 2 Corinthians 10:3–5,

> *We are human, but we don't wage war as humans do. We use God's mighty weapons, not worldly weapons, to knock down strongholds of human reasoning and to destroy false arguments. We destroy every proud obstacle that keeps people from knowing God. We capture their rebellious thoughts and teach them to obey Christ.*

More than ever, I realized this was a war that would not be won by human effort. I knew I could not sit around and only hope for her to change. I had to war with this Word. Contained in these verses I saw the co-laboring work of intercession between the Holy Spirit and me. I had no power in the flesh to fight this kind of enemy. But the verses revealed that God had given me weapons to knock down the imaginations, lies, and rebellious thoughts inside of Lindsey's mind.

With God's Word in my hand and on my tongue, I began to wage war for the reconciliation of Lindsey back to God, back to Casey, back to Analeise and Katie, and back to her sister and me. I took these verses literally. Walking to and fro on the dirt road behind my house, with no one to hear me except God and the wildlife living in the woods, the words exploded out of my mouth, "Lindsey, in the Name of Jesus, I pull down the imaginations in your mind! You have the mind of Christ!

"With the authority of the Word of God, I declare the destruction of every lie of the enemy! You know the truth, and the truth will set you free!

"Lindsey, by the power of the blood of Jesus, I declare this rebellion and proud spirit bows its knees to the authority of the will of God!

"I use the Name, the blood, and the Word to pull down these strongholds, imaginations, and lies. I destroy every obstacle, every wrong relationship and influence that is keeping Lindsey from God. I pull down these rebellious thoughts and declare Lindsey will obey Christ!"

Then I was led to 2 Corinthians 5:18–20,

And God has given us the task of reconciling people to him. For God was in Christ, reconciling the world to himself, no longer counting people's sins against them. And he gave us this wonderful message of reconciliation. So we are Christ's ambassadors; God is making his appeal through us. We speak for Christ when we plead, "Come back to God!"

I came away with a greater understanding of these verses. I saw myself as an ambassador of Christ here to decree His will on the earth as it is in Heaven. I realized through this word that when I opened my mouth, raised my voice, and declared God's Word, He was making His appeal through me! I wasn't praying on my own. I was speaking for Christ when I was pleading in intercession, "Come back to God!"

Again, I took this literally. I went outside on my front porch and allowed the Holy Spirit to make His appeal through me. I called for Lindsey as I would have if she were once again a child who was needing to get right back to the security and safety of our home. I raised my voice and called out to her with everything I had inside me, naturally and spiritually. With faith and passion I cried, "Lindsey, come back to God! *Lindsey, come back to God!"*

It did not matter that she lived in another city over an hour away. I knew there was no distance in the realm of the spirit. I was not dealing with the natural realm anyway. I was in a place where there was no time or space. I was co-laboring with Christ, declaring the will of the Father, and the Holy Spirit was taking my words to wherever she was. She could not hear me in the natural realm, but she was being stirred in her spirit by something she did not even understand.

This form of prayer became a constant, unrelenting pattern. I did not know how long it would take or how it would happen, but I knew that His Word would not return void. Someday, Lindsey would come back to God and His will for her life.

Getting My Hopes Up

December 1, 2014, I was heavily burdened. Kneeling on the floor of my living room, I cried out to God. Convinced He was present and hearing me, I called out, "Father, go get Lindsey, today. Let the scales fall from her eyes. Cause her to see truth! Today, God! Let it be today, God!"

I had been praying awhile when I heard Him say, "Go to Second Kings, chapter four. Read the story of the Shunamite woman."

He was taking me back to the familiar story. I figured, if He told me to read it again, there must be something He wanted me to see and hear that I hadn't seen or heard before.

Once again, I opened my Bible and began to read about this woman and her awesome testimony. I made mental notes as I read, reminding myself of her story's details.

She was a wealthy woman who loved and feared God.

She recognized Elisha was a prophet sent from the Lord, and her heart was pricked to do something to honor him.

What did she do? She prepared meals for him and even had a room built in her home to house him when he came through town.

After many visits to her home, enjoying the hospitality of this woman and her husband, Elisha wanted to do something to honor them in return. When Elisha asked her to tell him what he could do for her, she kindly replied, "No, my family takes good care of me."

In today's vernacular, she'd be saying, "No, thanks. We're good. Everything's okay."

Then, Elisha's servant, Gehazi, spoke up and said, "She doesn't have a son, and her husband is an old man."

Wasn't that kind of Gehazi? "She's barren and married to an old dude." Nice.

As I read the familiar story, in the back of my mind I thought, *I'll read through this quickly so I can get to the part where Elisha raises her son from the dead. Last time, God was pointing out the portion of scripture about recovering everything. This time, He's reminding me of resurrection life. That is probably why the Lord has asked me to read this.* I just love it when I think I have God all figured out and then He blows my mind!

Still kneeling on the floor, I read on. Suddenly, the most unexpected thing happened. When I read verse sixteen, I actually heard the words as if they were being spoken to me: "Next year at this time you will be holding a son in your arms."

Immediately, I knew what my Father was telling me. He wasn't telling me I was going to be the next Sarah! He was talking to me about Lindsey. My mind and heart knew God was not only going to restore the marriage, but Lindsey and Casey were going to have another baby, and the baby would be a son!

Our Father is amazing! There I was, calling on God to rescue and save my daughter. I was praying for her marriage and life to be restored. Lindsey's having a baby wasn't on my prayer list! I wasn't even thinking about it. Apparently, however, God was.

Here I was wanting the reconciliation of the marriage which was looking more impossible by the day. God didn't seem concerned at all about the worsening circumstances. He was happily planning the future and letting me in on it. I was so blessed by that.

Casey had always wanted a son, but Lindsey hadn't been interested in having any more children, and even before she left, she had made that abundantly clear.

Taking a pen, I underlined 2 Kings 4:16 in my Bible and wrote beside it the date, 12/1/14. In the margin, I wrote these words, "I will hold a son."

I also wrote this in my journal:

I'm going to write something interesting I heard tonight.

Out of 2 Kings 4:16, "Next year at this time you will be holding a son in your arms."

I believe I will hold Lindsey and Casey's son in my arms, and he will be greatly used of God with a powerful Nazarite anointing on him to preach the Gospel.

I believe. Yes, I believe.

I pondered this promise in my heart and began to pray intensely for the promised boy. The word seemed far-fetched, so I was very hesitant to share it with anyone.

Finally, a few weeks later, for the sake of agreement, I shared it with Pam Barnett.

We were sitting at my kitchen table, and I said, "Pam, I have something to tell you, but you can't tell anyone."

She nodded affirmatively.

"Not only is Lindsey and Casey's marriage going to be restored, but they are going to have a son!"

I could tell she was a little shocked, so I told her the story of how I received the word. She heard it through the ears of faith and became as excited as I was. With her hands holding her face, she replied, "Oh, Karen! This is amazing! They're going to have a baby!"

We began to pray with the power that comes from agreeing together on a word from God! We declared this word to be established in the earth.

Confirmation

A couple of weeks later, I had invited Leah Accord and Pam to join me for a time of prayer in my living room. Leah has a violent faith and an amazingly keen ear to hear the Voice of God. As we were interceding for Lindsey, Leah stopped and said, "Earlier today, I was with Analeise, and she said to me, 'I'm going to have a baby brother!'"

Pam and I looked at each other with eyes that looked like saucers!

I had told no one but Pam about this secret that God had shared with me. Leah had no idea what she was saying!

Leah continued, "I believe that not only are Lindsey and Casey getting back together, they are also going to have another baby, and it's going to be a boy!"

The Spirit of God fell upon Leah, and she began to wail in intercession. I remember her praying, "The womb is calling! The womb is calling!" She continued for some time to pray and prophesy about the baby.

We continued in prayer until the burden lifted. We had prayed for hours.

Around midnight, Leah stood up and said, "I'm going to Walmart to buy boy clothes!" And that's just what she did!

A bit later, she returned to my house with clothes, blankets, pacifiers, bibs, and an adorable teddy bear—all for this little boy who wasn't yet a glint in his parents' eyes! I placed the "boy gifts" up on the shelves inside my closet so that I would see them each day as a reminder of the promise of God. These items were for me "the substance of things hoped for and the evidence of things unseen."

It was a few weeks later before I felt released to tell Leah about the word God had given me on December 1. The fact that she did not know what I already knew only made her acts and words of faith more precious to me.

There were many times that the intercession focused on this child God had promised was coming. I spent much time praying that he would come at the *right* time. I prayed over him the prophetic word God had spoken concerning him, declaring this word of God to be manifested in the earth.

As the situation with Lindsey grew worse, and the fulfillment of a promised son seemed further and further out of reach, I continued to hold on to the promise God had given me. My unrelenting confession became, "It will be as God has said, 'I *will* hold a son, Lindsey and Casey's son.'"

Several months after receiving this promise and contending for it in prayer, a man of God from St. Louis, Missouri, stopped by the Ramp to visit me. His name was Pastor Roy Boyer. He moved in a strong prophetic anointing. He knew nothing about the promise of a son. Neither did he know the details of Lindsey's situation, though he understood I was in some sort of crisis with her. For that, he had been praying.

As we were sitting in the green room at the Ramp, talking about the restoration I was believing for, he said, "You know this is about a child that is to be born."

Shocked by his comment, I replied, "I do."

Then he proceeded to confirm the word God had given me almost a year before. I was so grateful for the kindness of the Father to encourage me with yet another word.

A Feather Falls

Later in December 2014, I was struggling with holding on to my hope. It seemed each time I would hear of another situation regarding Lindsey, it was as if something had knocked the breath out of me. I requested Leigh Smalley, a dear friend and woman of faith, and Pam come over to the house to pray with me. They came, and we prayed—or should I say, they prayed—in the Millhouse.

The pressure was weighing down on me so heavily that I could hardly speak, much less pray. However, I wanted to be in God's Presence, and I knew my friends could help me get there.

Pam began to lift her voice, "Jesus, we welcome You. We want You and need You. Speak to us, Lord. We are here, and we are listening."

While we tarried, we drifted into worship, and after that Pam began to lead me in prayer, literally telling me the words to say. I repeated them.

As she led me deeper into prayer, she asked, "Karen, do you see a wall?"

"Yes. It is a big, thick, ancient wall, and Lindsey is behind it," I told her.

"Ask Jesus to give you a tool to bring the wall down," Pam instructed me.

I repeated, "Jesus, give me a tool to bring down this wall."

There, in the quiet, I waited. *What would I see? An ax? A sledgehammer? Maybe He would provide me with a bulldozer!* I wondered, my heart starting to feel expectant.

Then, to my amazement, I saw it! It was a feather. You could have knocked me over. I saw a simple white feather.

It took me so off-guard that I began to laugh. Pam began to laugh, too, even though she didn't know what I was finding so funny. She asked, "What did He give you?"

"A feather!" I answered. "He gave me a feather because He wants me to know how easy this is!"

Oh, His word came to me once more, and it was enough to give me hope. Rejoicing in the beauty and simplicity of the revelation, I tucked the simple promise away deep in my heart and told no one about it, and neither did Pam nor Leigh speak of it to anyone.

Reminded

Seven months passed. I had attempted to talk to Lindsey, and it hadn't ended well. She was cold and uninterested in anything I had to say. She was adrift, moving further away from us.

I found myself sitting in my living room, desperate to hear from God. I thought we were at a turning point or at least getting somewhere, but we weren't. Per the pattern I was beginning to experience, things seemed to get worse right after I had seen evidence of some progress.

With unspeakable questions and the voices of fear swirling around me, I heard the familiar *ding* from my phone. I picked it up. It was a text from Leah.

These were the words I read, "Remember, as easy as a feather, and every wall comes crashing down!"

Actually, instead of the word *feather*, she had used a picture of a white feather like the one I had seen earlier in the Millhouse!

The words in front of me resuscitated my heart, especially since Leah hadn't been in the Millhouse that December night. She had absolutely no idea I had received the same word from God.

Everything about this was God, the words and the picture of the feather. I wanted to run around my house and scream, "There is a God in Heaven, and He keeps on texting me on my phone!"

How faithful God was to me. His very personal commitment to see me through was evidenced time and time again. It rejoiced my heart!

Only moments before, I was hysterically fighting with fear and panic, and then it seemed as though my Father came into the room, knelt in front of me, gently shook me by my shoulders, snapped His fingers in my face, and said, "Remember! Remember! Remember what I said, Karen! Don't forget My word to you! I still remember what I told you in the Millhouse. This is not hard for Me. This is as easy as a feather. This wall will come crashing down."

How wonderful to be reminded by God—that He hadn't forgotten His word to me, and therefore, I shouldn't forget it either. He was teaching me how to increase my faith by remembering. He wanted me to remember what He had promised and to remember what He had done already for me in the past. This was one of the ways He taught His disciples.

In Matthew 16:7–10, the disciples were concerned that they had brought no bread to eat. Jesus' response to them was, "Don't you remember the 5,000 I fed with five loaves, and the baskets of leftovers you picked up? Or the 4,000 I fed with seven loaves and the large assets of leftovers you picked up?"

In the middle of my need, I was encouraged to remember what He had done already. Years ago, I often sang a song with these lyrics, "He'll do it again. He'll do it again. Just take a look at where you are now, and where you've been. Hasn't He always come through for you? He's the same God as then. You may not know how, you may not know when, but He'll do it again!"

Lesson learned.

I have no words for where I am. They do not exist.

Yet my Father understands even the groan of my spirit. Even the silence of it.

How do I let go or hold on?

I do not know what to do or how to do it.

I do not understand. At. All.

God, please help me in this place.

Where is Your peace? Where is Your joy?

Maybe I was wrong thinking I could help.

Here I am, feeling used and confused.

Yet . . . I trust in God.

Yet . . . I worship God.

God is my Father.

I look to Him.

Father, where are Your?

—January 21, 2015

Chapter Eight

. . . . .

VICTORY PROMISED

2014 was almost over. I was flying to Dallas to be on Daystar. On the way, I received some terrible news about Lindsey. The pressure was overwhelming. Each breath I breathed was labored. I picked up my phone and typed out a sentence to text to Pam: "Pam, I want this to be over."

As I typed, I felt the weight of each letter. In fact, it felt as if it took me a lifetime to type those seven words. I meant it. I wanted this to be over.

Later that evening, I arrived at my hotel and, sometime in the morning hours, managed to fall asleep. I dreamed that I was standing in a room that was enclosed by windows all around. Inside the room was an empty indoor swimming pool. And standing with me in the room were my mother and my sister.

In the dream, I began to sing an old song I remember hearing in church as a child, a hymn by Isaac Watts. In perfect three-part harmony, Mother and Janet joined me,

And when the battle's over, we shall wear a crown! Yes, we shall wear a crown! Yes, we shall wear a crown! And when

the battle's over, we shall wear a crown in the new Jerusalem.
Wear a crown (wear a crown), wear a crown (wear a crown),
wear a bright and shining crown. And when the battle's over,
we shall wear a crown in the new Jerusalem.

After we sang the song through once, Mother said, "Sing it again!" So, I raised the key, and we sang it again! As we sang, I saw Casey walk up to us, and the dream ended.

When I woke, I knew I had heard God's response to the text I had sent Pam earlier. God was telling me, "It's going to be over, Karen, and when it is over, *you* will wear a crown!" It was a word from God declaring my victory! I was so encouraged by this.

A month later, I felt led to drive to Cleveland, Tennessee, to hear Chuck Pierce minister at Dwelling Place Church. It would be good to see my friend Judy Jacobs again. Since I was a bit late, I had to walk in front of everyone to take the front-row seat that Judy had saved for me.

As soon as Chuck Pierce took the podium, the first thing he said was, "Karen, when you came in tonight, I saw a crown of laurel leaves on your head."

I understood immediately what the Lord was saying to me. I knew the laurel leaf crown was a symbol of victory. I knew God was confirming His word to me!

The very next week, I was in a Ramp conference. A dear lady I did not know came up to my daughter Lauren, and said, "Tell your mother that during this conference I have been seeing crowns on her head." Then she gave Lauren a beautiful necklace with a crown on it to give to me as a gift!

For the next several months, I wore the crown necklace every day to remind me of the victory I knew was mine.

Crowned

By April 2, 2015, I found myself battling with exhaustion and fear. It was late at night, and I didn't feel like I even had the strength to explain to Pam the battle I was in. I decided to send her a simple picture of a crown—a good reminder for both of us that the victory was ours.

I googled crowns, and after looking at about one hundred different kinds, I found a beautiful gold crown and texted the picture with no caption. I thought it would speak for itself. After all, Pam knew all about the crown dream and prophetic words, so I knew she would know what it meant.

Two hours later, I received a text from Jon Potter. He is a prophet who pastors in Birmingham, Alabama. I read his text. To my amazement, it was a picture of a crown. Half of the crown was beautiful, the other half a crown of thorns. The caption on the picture read, "A lot can happen in three days."

I was just blown away! Once again, God had responded to the text I had just sent of the crown. He had sent me a text back with His own crown on it, and a mysterious word—"A lot can happen in three days."

I took the word at face value and believed that in three days Lindsey was coming home! Even though it was midnight, I called Pam and told her what had just happened. Both of us rejoiced and believed this was it. I figured up the days. *Today is April 2nd. That means in three days, it will be April 5th.*

Lindsey is coming home this weekend. And even better yet, it will be Easter. Three days until a resurrection!

That weekend, things did seem different—amazingly different!

I took every opportunity I could to be with Lindsey. On that Friday, I took her and the girls to dinner in Tupelo, Mississippi. We saw the new Cinderella movie that had just been released. It was kind of hilarious, actually. I thought the young handsome prince in the movie had an uncanny resemblance to Casey. And I kept wondering if Lindsey noticed. I loved it when Analeise said, "The prince looks like my daddy!"

Lindsey smiled and nodded in agreement.

On the way home, she talked about Casey, reliving old memories of when they were first married, and laughing about how much he favored Cinderella's prince. We even googled pictures of the two of them to compare. This was so unusual for her to even be speaking of Casey in a casual conversation! My heart was beating with excitement and hope.

Two days later, it was Katie's birthday. We held her party in the Ramp green room. It was like a miracle was happening. Lindsey had gone over the top decorating for the party. She seemed anxious and sort of excited for Casey to get there. When he did arrive, I noticed she was making every effort to say something so he would hear or notice. Then to top it all off, she gave him a gift! She knew his favorite candy was Reese's peanut butter cups, and she had even frozen them, just the way he liked them.

This is it! Lindsey is coming home! It's going to be like Jon Potter said, "A lot can happen in three days!" And this is the third day! My thoughts were full of expectancy.

The next few days were spent with minimal but nice contact with her. She even invited Casey to a birthday dinner for Lauren. I was so encouraged and thought surely this was the beginning of the miracle we had been believing for.

But it was not to be.

The morning after the birthday dinner, with a heart full of hope, Casey went by her house to pick up the girls. When she came out to Casey's car, she was wearing the hat of the man she was currently seeing.

In a subtle, yet bold defiance, Lindsey once again took the dagger and lunged it into Casey's hopeful heart. It seemed as though in an instant she had reverted back to that horrible pit of darkness and hard resolve.

The thought of her being in yet another relationship with another man was almost more than I could bear.

How could she do this to Casey?

I knew some of the pain that Casey was feeling because I too had known the unspeakable sorrow of an unfaithful spouse. I always felt that, in some ways, it would have been easier to bury a spouse that you knew loved you than to have your trust shattered, your covenant broken, and your intimacy shared.

It is so hard to ride the roller coaster of hope and despair. I knew Casey hated it as much as I did. I continued to pray not only for Lindsey, but especially for Casey. With all my heart, I prayed for God to give him grace to keep hope alive in his heart. I prayed that his love for her would not die and that, somehow, God would heal the unspeakable pain in his heart.

I held on to the promise God had given me. Someday, this battle would be over, and when it was, I would wear a crown.

How do you describe the most painful and hardest day of your life?

I don't have words, really.

Swirling. Trying. Exhausted.

Beyond tears, yet I want to cry. And cry. And cry.

Yet it wouldn't help or change anything.

So I feel all this pent-up emotion.

Desperate. Desperate in believing.

Searching. Want to scream. And scream and scream.

Yet it wouldn't help or change anything, either.

So I wait. And wonder. And wander. And wait.

—March 19, 2015

Chapter Nine

.....

CONFIRMING SIGNS

I was learning a lot throughout this journey. I was hearing the Voice speak to me in many jaw-dropping ways. He used words—those from His Word, His Voice, and others—and images—those in dreams, in nature, and even on the Internet. And what that did to my faith, I don't know if I have the words to express it. All I can say is that each word, insight, or image ratcheted up faith in me. Even though circumstances or news of Lindsey's present life assailed me, God was gracious to provide the very thing I needed to boost my faith.

God knew how to get my attention. And once He did, I kept looking and listening for Him. Several times, Jesus repeated this statement, "Let him who has ears to hear, *hear* what the Spirit is saying!" I understood like never before that God was speaking, and I needed to *hear* Him for my situation.

Jeremiah 33:3 says, "Call unto me, and *I will answer you!*" When I prayed or asked God a question, I grew to *expect* Him to answer! Even as I went about my daily activities, I started to live in a watchful expectancy that God was going to speak to me.

Trust me, there was enough noise all around me, so many voices fighting for my attention. Thankfully, God used some very unusual words and images that made me come aside and see what it was He was trying to tell me.

I let God be God in my life. I didn't try to tell Him how to speak to me. I soon realized He wasn't going to talk to me in the ways in which I was most familiar or comfortable. Yet, I have to say, He was speaking my language, for He helped me understand what He was saying and showing me. Others around me didn't always get it, but some did and stood with me. And that was the important thing, because I was a mother doing battle for her daughter.

Some people thought it was strange when I said, "I heard God," or "I heard the Voice speak to me." Not me. I thought it was strange when someone who claimed to be a Christian said she hadn't heard the Voice. Jesus said, in John 10:27, "My sheep *know My voice*"!

The entire Bible was written by, and about, men and women who were led by the Voice. If my encounters with God seemed strange to anyone, I couldn't change that. The Bible is replete with encounters, both awe-inspiring and absolutely wild, that people had with God.

He spoke to them through a burning bush, the stars in the heavens, a hand that mysteriously appeared and started writing on the wall, night dreams, angelic visitations, and visions. Once, God even spoke to a man through the donkey he was riding! Now that would get my attention! So I just couldn't think it was strange when God used a reptile in distress to speak to me.

The Turtle

Pam and I were on Prayer Mountain. We had been praying for some time when I felt to declare that it was time for a "turnaround" for Lindsey and Casey. Pam and I stood together, facing the same direction, and decreed every word from God we felt in our spirits to declare.

Soon, we began to prophesy to the situation itself and shout, "Turn around!"

We said loudly, "We declare today, in the Name of Jesus, Lindsey is going to turn around! We declare, in the Name of Jesus, this marriage is going to turn around!"

Each time we said the word *turnaround* or the phrase *turn around,* we physically turned around. We did this as a prophetic sign of what we were declaring and believing for. We prayed this way full of faith and with all of our hearts.

When we were finished, we went to the buggy and prepared to head back down Prayer Mountain to go home. Halfway down, I stopped the buggy and asked God to "give us a sign of His favor." I was asking for a sign that He had indeed heard us and was answering our prayer.

We continued to ride down the hill, through the future site of Camp Ramp that follows the winding beauty of Williams Creek. We were about to come to "The Rock Hole." This happens to be another one of my favorite places on Earth. Here, the creek opens up wide enough to accommodate the very large rock that lies in the water. It is here we have baptized thousands of young men and women who come to our summer conferences.

As Pam and I reached this beautiful place, I decided to stop the buggy, only for a moment, to listen to the water as it swept across the rocks. Within a few seconds, something caught my eye. It was lying on the other side of the creek beside the water. It was a strange color of yellow, cream, and orange.

I said, "Look, Pam. What is that?"

Then, it moved.

Startled, I realized what it was. It was a very large turtle that was upside down.

I said, "Oh, no, Pam! It's on its back and can't turn over."

Before I could even make a plan to cross the creek to come to the turtle's rescue, right before our eyes, it flipped over! It was as though an unseen hand took it and turned it over in an instant!

Standing there staring with our mouths hanging open, we couldn't believe our eyes. Needing confirmation, we looked at each other. And without hesitation shouted simultaneously, *"Turn around!"*

Here was the sign we had asked for on our journey down Prayer Mountain.

In an instant, both of us jumped off the buggy and started running and shouting at the top of our lungs. That's the kind of women we are. We've got to move when we see God move.

God *had* spoken, and we knew it. He had heard my prayer and answered it before I could even arrive home!

The Alligator

A few months later, Pam's son, Daniel, had a dream. In the dream, he saw an alligator inside the wall of his apartment. He was concerned about what to do.

Suddenly, the wall began to shake and crack open. Pam was there with him and said, "Don't be afraid. This thing is about to be exposed."

Crash, without warning, the very large alligator fell out of the wall and began to crawl down the hall toward the front door. There was a little girl standing outside the door. Daniel knew the intent of the alligator was to take her.

As it reached the door, Daniel saw his mother stand in front of the gator and say, "I command you to give back what you stole from me!"

Clutched in the gator's claws was a hundred-dollar bill. Reluctantly, the gator gave the money to Pam.

When Daniel saw what his mother had done, he also said to the alligator, "I command you to give me what you have stolen from me!"

Reluctantly again, the gator handed Daniel a hundred-dollar bill. The dream ended.

Within two weeks of this dream, four other people from our Ramp Church had dreams involving alligators. None of them knew about the other's dream until each began sharing the dreams with me. I noted the specificity of detail in each dream and kept that to myself, pondering what God was saying to us.

I understood the crocodile, dragon, or leviathan represented a cruel and ominous enemy in Scripture. At times, that enemy was depicted as coming against the people of God. Whether it was a croc, gator, or leviathan we were dealing with, one thing I knew: We had to wage war against it—that's what I believed God was wanting us to do.

My prayer team and I began to specifically target that thing in prayer. Using the authority of Jesus' Name, we declared the victory of Jesus over it and continued in prevailing prayer until we felt a release.

A few days later, Pam, her husband, Kevin, and I traveled together to Chattanooga. I was headed to minister in a church there. It was May of 2015.

Ding, I looked down at my phone. It was Lauren. She messaged me a news article. The title of the article read, "World's biggest American gator caught in Alabama River."

The huge gator had not been found in the typical marshes of Louisiana or Florida; it had been killed near Camden, Alabama. And it had been taken to be displayed in Montgomery, the capital of the state where we were bombarding Heaven!

A picture of the gator was posted in the article. It didn't even look real. It looked like a monster of sorts; in fact, the article referred to the reptile as a "monster gator." And its exact weight was 1,011 pounds. That's right. Not 1,010 or 1,012 pounds. It had to be *1,011* pounds because God wanted to remind us of His *111!*

Lauren, Pam, and I knew we had been given the victory over this spirit. It had been defeated! We simply needed to keep praying because it was working.

I discovered much later on that the gator had been killed by a woman in August of 2014. That gator had been taken out before we prayed against the alligator others around me had seen in their dreams.

Apparently, after the gator was killed, it was taken to the taxidermist and readied to go on display. That gator and the huntress who took it out had been showcased throughout the state, finally ending up in Montgomery where the gator was put more permanently on display.

This reminded me of Colossians 2:15, Jesus "disarmed the spiritual rulers and authorities. He shamed them publicly by his victory over them on the cross."

Jesus defeated our enemies and paraded them for the world to see as a defeated foe. To me and Pam and Lauren, "the world's biggest American alligator" showcased in Montgomery and throughout our home state was just another way for Jesus to *"make a show"* of His great victory!

When Pam and I received the message on my phone, we had Kevin pull the car over on the highway so that we could get out and run, dance, and shout! And we sure did!

The Bridge

Miriam Logan, one of the young ladies on my ministry team, Chosen, came to me with a dream she had concerning Lindsey and Casey.

In the dream, she saw a large, deep body of water. It was dark blue, almost black, in color. It had large pieces of ice floating on top. Standing in the water was a large bridge, but the middle of it was out. She could see Lindsey on one side of the bridge and Casey on the other.

As the dream progressed, she saw Casey jump into the water, attempting to swim to where Lindsey was. However, the distance was too far and the water too cold. He swam as far as he could until his body began to freeze. He gave in to the exhaustion and instead swam to a nearby island. He stood on the shore, almost lifeless as a little girl, that changed from Analeise to Katie, ran up to him crying, "Daddy! Daddy!" Then Miriam awoke.

I was troubled by the dream—by the missing part of the bridge. It seemed to be revealing where things stood presently with Lindsey's and Casey's relationship without offering me any insight or wisdom as to how to pray or what to do for the bridge to be made whole. I knew I had to commit the dream and the missing part of the bridge to Jesus.

A few days later, unaware of Miriam's dream, my friend Jon Potter texted me very early in the morning:

> Good morning, awakened at 4:27 this morning, and I saw an image of an incomplete bridge. There was a gap in the middle. I then saw what I could only describe as an inverted symbol of the Greek letter pi coming down from heaven and completing the missing piece of the bridge. I spent an hour online looking for anything that resembled that vision but couldn't find it. I took an image of a bridge, and through a photo editor software, I tried to draw out what I saw. I looked up the word pi and found out it is the first Greek symbol in the word pistis which is the Greek word for faith. The interpretation I got was that GREAT FAITH is coming down from Heaven that is going to be a connector between two things that have not happened yet.

Then he sent me a picture of the bridge that he created as a representation of what he had seen in the vision. At the very center of the bridge, there was this gap—the missing part Miriam had seen in her dream and Jon had seen in his vision. Now, it was plain for me to see. I was blown away that God appeared to be answering the question left by the first dream—namely, what needed to happen for the bridge to be made whole? I was stunned that God answered that question with such clarity, telling me great faith coming from Heaven would bridge the gap.

God was speaking to me to keep believing the word He was speaking over Casey and Lindsey. Faith comes by hearing and hearing by the Word of God!

I received this message from God and kept believing.

Stars

I've always loved the study of the universe. Thankfully, I live in the country and have a wonderful view of the handiwork of God in the night sky. Many nights I stand outside in the dark, taking in as many stars as my eyes can see, captured by the thought that my Father knows "each star" by name!

In June of 2015, I began to notice two stars in particular that dominated the night sky, demanding my attention. I was totally intrigued by their brightness and noticed every night they seemed to move closer to each other. I began to use them as a focus of prayer. "Lord, just like these two stars, move Lindsey and Casey closer and closer to each other. Every day, Lord, draw their hearts together."

I shared my intrigue with Pam so she could join me in my night prayer as we looked at these two unusual stars.

One night, I was alone with the Lord, looking heavenward. I said, "Lord, You know that, to me, these two stars represent Lindsey and Casey. Father, it would just be so wonderful if these two stars moved so close together that they became one!" It was my mother-heart for my children to be united again that prompted me to be so specific in my request.

Later that same night, I happened to hear a news anchor on the evening news announce the names of these two stars—actually, they were planets. The anchor continued to say, "Tonight, these two planets are going to come so close to each other that it will be as though they are one."

Oh, my, did I just hear that?! I could hardly contain myself. God had heard my prayer and answered me.

Now, I knew these events took place on a star cycle that could be predicted by astronomers. For me, that just made it all the more wonderful. It said to me, when God created the universe and set the stars into motion, He knew that, on this June night in the year 2015, there would be a mother named Karen, in Hamilton, Alabama, who needed encouragement. He knew I would pray that prayer on that night, so as He created the universe and the cycle of the stars, He made arrangements to answer my prayer.

I know I shouldn't have been surprised, and I wasn't necessarily surprised. I was more in awe. That He—the Creator of the universe, the One who spoke and it was—would speak to me was too marvelous for words!

"I love You, my Father," I said to Him in response.

All of this was God assuring me that He would keep His promises.

I commit myself to You.

I have made many mistakes on this journey with You for my daughter.

I ask forgiveness for each one.

Today, I find myself at a place of another altar.

Another surrender. Another letting go.

Help me know how.

In this moment, I surrender.

I trust You. Help me know how to trust You.

You absolutely deserve to be trusted.

Help me to let go, Father. Help me.

I am exhausted. I don't know how to rest.

I'm sorry.

The only things I know I can say right now is . . .

I worship You. I love You.

You are still Lord. And always will be.

—September 30, 2015

I have released Lindsey to God.

Last Friday she said some things to me that only Jesus can heal.

I've never felt anything like that pain.

I've never cried that deeply over anything.

Since then, I've been in a different place.

Not even sure if it's good or bad, but I do know it is necessary.

The pain has to stop. I am stepping off the pendulum.

I have resolved in my heart a few things . . .

God has not failed me. God has not forsaken me.

God does not lie. God is good and perfect and right in all His ways.

God is worthy to be trusted.

Over the past three years, I have received many words from God . . .

I believe them.

Here is where I am regarding my promises . . .

I give them back to God in trust. I cannot make them come to pass.

Whatever God has spoken will come to pass.

Yes. It will be as He has said it will be.

If I have misunderstood what He was saying to me,

He will give me grace to face whatever I must face.

There is NO accusation against God. He. Does. Not. Lie.

I am going inside God.

To my safe place. To my refuge.

To a place of healing. To a place of rest.

And there . . . I will find my place of victory.

For in Him . . . I will always triumph.

—November 3, 2015

Chapter Ten

· · · · ·

LOOKING TO JESUS

By the fall of 2015, I could hardly believe I was still in this battle. Lindsey had moved to another city, gotten her own apartment, and started a new job. She was also involved in yet another relationship.

Casey was trying to carry on with life and ministry the best he could as a single dad. I knew he was constantly in a battle with his own heart and mind.

How could he continue to take one let down after another? How long can he hold on to even a thread of hope? I understood his faith and person were being stretched and greatly tested.

I had to face the facts. Lazarus was going to die.

To be honest, during this season, I didn't even want to read the story of Lazarus. I didn't want it to come to that. I wasn't sure if I had the faith to believe something totally dead could ever live again. I realized I needed to know how to keep believing when things seemed to be over—when the corpse of what was had started to stink!

The Tomb

How is it possible to still have faith when it appears all is lost? That was the question I was asking myself.

I picked up my Bible, walked into this story, and found my answer. I read:

> *When Jesus arrived at Bethany, he was told that Lazarus had already been in his grave for four days. Bethany was only a few miles down the road from Jerusalem and many of the people had come to console Martha and Mary in their loss. When Martha got word that Jesus was coming, she went to meet him. But Mary stayed in the house. Martha said to Jesus, "Lord, if only you had been here, my brother would not have died. But even now I know that God will give you whatever you ask."*
>
> *—John 11:17–22*

There they were. Those two little words—*even now!*

Although Martha was hurt and disappointed that Jesus had not come when she so desperately needed Him to be there, she did not allow her faith to die with Lazarus. In essence, Martha was saying, "I know he's dead, Jesus, but *even now,* with Lazarus inside the tomb, God will give you whatever You ask.

"*Even now,* though it is completely hopeless and impossible in the natural.

"*Even now,* though everyone else has given up and accepted the finality of the situation.

"*Even now,* Jesus, I believe God will still give You whatever You ask."

Hers wasn't a lot of faith, only two little words, but it was all Jesus needed! Jesus immediately responded to her faith with His own declaration, "Your brother will rise again" (John 11:23).

Martha quickly said with her natural understanding of Scripture, "Yes, he will rise again on the last day" (see v. 24).

Her faith was not perfect faith, but Jesus never said we had to have perfect faith. He said we only needed a little bit of faith, and with it we could move a mountain!

Her natural response did not stop Jesus. He had already heard her *even now* faith, so He said, "Take Me to the tomb!"

When they arrived at the tomb, with Martha's trembling heart standing beside Him, He said, "Roll the stone aside" (John 11:39).

Once again, Martha's faith wobbled as she said, "But, Lord, he's been dead four days, and by now he is stinking!"

This time the words of Jesus shook her faith into focus, "Martha! Didn't I tell you if you would *believe,* you would see the glory of God?"

This time, she had no response because she knew, down deep in her heart, her *even now* moment had come!

Shaking from head to toe and with her heart beating out of her chest, she heard God shout, *"Lazarus, come forth!"*

With her eyes opened wide and locked on the darkness inside the tomb, she saw something moving.

What's that? Could it be? she wondered, her eyes squinting to decipher what she saw.

There, the silhouette of a man wrapped in the grave clothes that she had prepared finally emerged from the tomb. It was Lazarus—the one she loved, the one she had prayed and believed for! He was alive, fully alive!

Weeping, she ran to embrace him. In a moment, inexpressible sorrow had turned to unspeakable joy!

In the midst of the glorious chaos, as the family of Lazarus surrounded him with tears, love, and laughter, Martha turned aside and saw Jesus. He was standing with a beautiful smile on His face. He had done what He loved to do best. He had brought life to the dead and brought great glory to His Father.

With tears still streaming down her cheeks, she ran to Him. What more was there to say but *thank you.*

Although Jesus did not come when Martha thought He should, she didn't give up. She kept watching the road. When everyone else thought it was over, Martha kept a little faith alive, and it paid off.

Those two little words, *even now,* were the key that unlocked the tomb. Jesus just needed her to believe what He was saying more than what she was seeing.

I needed to be like Martha. I needed to keep on believing for Lindsey, her marriage, her family, and her ministry. I couldn't give up now. Even with the corpse of my hope lying inside the tomb and with everyone else "done gone and left" me with their flowers and pity, I could not leave the graveside just yet. Even if I were going to be the only one left, I was determined to set up camp outside of the tomb and keep watching the road. I didn't know when Jesus would get there, but I knew He was on His way!

A dead dream or a dead marriage would be no match for the One who is the Resurrection and the Life!

Heaven's Courtroom

September 30, 2015, it was my birthday. It happened to fall on a Wednesday night, the time of the midweek service at the Ramp. Even though Casey was preaching, I asked Lindsey to come to the service to join me since it was my birthday. I wanted her in the room. It had been so long since she had sat in the Ramp for a service. She had poured so much of her own life into the place that I thought it would be good to have her remember what it was like.

Thankfully, she came. She sat in the middle section beside one of her friends.

As usual, Casey preached an incredible word. With everything inside me, I was praying Lindsey's heart would be softened to see and hear him again, doing what he was so obviously called and gifted to do.

When the service was over, she found a reason to leave as quickly as she possibly could. However, I was still feeling hopeful and thankful that she had actually come. Before I left, I wanted to talk with Casey for a few minutes, so I joined him in his car in the Ramp parking lot. Both of us were wondering what was going on inside her heart after having been in the service. It didn't take long to find out.

As we were sitting there chatting, Casey received a text from Lindsey letting him know that she had just sent him an email. This was unusual for her, so neither of us knew what to expect. We wondered if this might be the moment we had been waiting for.

After he read it to himself, he read it aloud to me. It was written from the place of her deepest bitterness. It was a scathing letter written with the intent to hurt and crush Casey as much as possible.

After he finished reading, there wasn't really a lot to be said by either of us. I went home hurting in my own heart but mostly concerned for the pain I knew Casey was feeling. He had held on for so long. I didn't know how much more of this he could take.

As is our birthday tradition, the girls and I had planned to go to Birmingham the next day to shop at The Summit, eat to our heart's content, and simply enjoy being together. But there was no joy in me. I didn't feel like pretending everything was all right and life was just moving on. I called the girls and cancelled the trip. I had to be alone. I had to go somewhere and find God. I wasn't sure where to go, so I packed my bags and started driving south.

The beach sounded good. A place to hear the water and think, that's what I needed. I headed towards Panama City Beach, Florida. Two very special friends of mine, Robert and Stacey Gay, pastor High Praise Church there. They recommended and blessed me with accommodations at a perfect little condo with a great ocean view.

For five days, I sat in the living room, watching dolphins and listening for God.

An incredible minister and personal friend of mine named Jane Hamon lived in Destin, Florida, not too far from where I was staying. After a few texts, we decided to meet for lunch. In her kindness, she and her husband allowed me to pour out the conflict of my soul, the struggle between the circumstances and the promises. I shared with them my experience on Prayer Mountain, when I entered the courtroom of Heaven and heard the *bang* of the gavel and the Judge of Heaven rule in my favor, "You will surely recover everything that was taken from you!"

As I was speaking, Jane asked me if I had ever heard of the book, *The Courtroom of Heaven* by Robert Henderson. I told her I had not. She began to share with me the revelation this man had received concerning the courtroom of Heaven, a place I had been, but didn't have complete revelation on as of yet.

The first moment I had to myself after lunch, I ordered the book online. Our discussion of the book so piqued my interest that I couldn't wait for the book to arrive. When I returned to the condo, I found the author's teaching online and began to listen to what turned into a personal word from God for me.

I discovered that Henderson also had a wayward son. He had spent two years praying for his son's healing and deliverance. During his journey, he began to understand that, when we contend in faith for something or pray over a period of time without receiving an answer, something is going on in the courtroom of Heaven. The accuser of the brethren is exercising a "legal right" to keep the answer from coming to us. In other words, there's something the accuser is accusing us of before God!

I jumped out of my bed and walked into the living room. As I stood there facing a beautiful ocean, I called for the convening of the courtroom of Heaven. I asked God to tell me anything the accuser had against me that could possibly be standing in the way of the manifestation of the promises God had given me. Throughout the night, I listened.

The next morning, as I packed my bags, I listened. It was on the way home, during the seven-hour drive alone with God, I finally heard Him speak. He spoke to me about a relationship with a couple that had been broken years ago.

When I first heard the word in my spirit, I thought, "But, God, I have done all I felt to do to make this right in my heart with You. I even attempted to make it right with them, but never heard a response. And now, You want me to try again?"

I couldn't stop thinking about it. Even though there was a lot of water under what used to be a bridge there, if the enemy was using this as an accusation against me, I wanted to deal with it.

Then I thought to myself, *If I knew I was going to die tomorrow, is there any relationship I would want restored before I slipped into eternity to face God?* There was no way I would want to leave this life without talking to this couple one more time. There was my answer.

Jesus said,

> So if you are presenting a sacrifice at the altar in the Temple and you suddenly remember that someone has something against you, leave your sacrifice there at that altar. Go and be reconciled to that person. Then come and offer your sacrifice to God.
>
> —*Matthew 5:23–24*

I thought of how many times I had gone to the Ramp to pray and taken Lindsey (by faith) to the altar and laid her there. Now it was time to leave my offering there and make a move toward reconciliation. I didn't care where the couple was or where I had to drive to get to them. I was going to find them. I didn't care about the details that had destroyed our relationship. There was no reason to go and bring those things back up. It was time to leave it all in the past and move forward. I didn't care who was right or wrong. All that mattered to me was making things right.

I found the couple's contact information and made the call. As we talked and cried, the Presence of God was manifested through the love and healing both of us could feel. When I hung up the phone, I felt a mountain *move*. One act of obedience had shifted something in the heavens and silenced the voice of the accuser.

I wish I could go away somewhere and rest. But I can't.

How do you rest when circumstances just bear down on you?

And when you manage to fall asleep, you wake up and they are still there . . . mocking, mocking.

Everything hurts right now.

It's strange.

Pictures hurt. Music hurts.

Reading hurts. Hope hurts.

Father. Father. Are You here?

Are You angry with me? What do You want me to do?

If I just dropped it all and let it all go, what would that even look like?

But that seems utterly impossible.

I don't know where to turn. Or what to do.

I just want this pressure to lift. This pain to stop.

I desire hope and faith to believe again.

And I desire to see the true manifestation of what is the word and will of God.

How far away from that am I?

Father, I am asking You for hope. True hope.

I do not want to believe or hope for anything that cannot be.

Father, I do not know how to do this. I am sorry.

I feel so tired. Hurt. Drained.

I don't even know if I'm hopeless or fearful or not.

I just know that I want to believe. I want to hope. I want faith.

I feel I'm at my end. I don't know if that's good or bad.

You and You alone know all these things.

You alone know the answers.

—November 12, 2015

Chapter Eleven

. . . . .

THE END OF
THE ROAD

The month of November began with the death of my father. Eight years prior, he had suffered a stroke. It led him into a horrible battle with Alzheimer's disease. He was a faithful husband to my mother and an incredible father to my sister and me.

Throughout my life, Daddy taught me to love the beauty and simplicity of country living. He was a man's man, strong and true to his word. He loved his tractor, his cows, and walking the old dirt road behind my house. Daddy loved the night sky, and he taught me to see God as the "great God of the universe." Although he always wanted to have a son, he was blessed with two daughters and five granddaughters! He loved his girls deeply and worked hard to make sure we were taken care of.

As a daughter, when you have a wonderful father, somehow you always feel safe in the world. Now, my daddy was gone. There would always be an empty place that only he could fill.

Even though I was relieved that his suffering was over and he was at perfect peace in the Presence of God, my heart was broken that I wouldn't be able to see him, touch him, or hear his voice, at least not again in this life.

The day of his funeral, we decided to take pictures of his immediate family and place them inside his jacket just before we saw him for the last time. Each of us walked up, lovingly placed our pictures with him, and said our goodbyes.

I was troubled by the fact that Casey's picture was not there with Lindsey's, especially knowing how much Dad loved both of them. So, when everyone had walked away, I quickly and quietly slipped back up to the casket, took a picture of the two of them together and placed it with him, by faith believing that they would once again be back together, even though presently the circumstances with Lindsey were unthinkable.

She had changed so much. She had hardened in her appearance. The effects of the lifestyle she had chosen was taking a toll on her in every way. She didn't look like the same person. Even her facial features looked chiseled, her eyes lacking the luster of a once buoyant personality. Her natural beauty was now hidden behind a darkness that was covering all of her. It was the defiant look of rebellion.

A few days after Dad's funeral, I received a call from Casey letting me know that, after almost two years of setbacks and delays, the day for mediation had come. He and Lindsey would finally settle the details of their divorce. For me, after having just finished all the funeral arrangements for my father, I felt as though I was having to watch as arrangements were being made for another funeral—for the death of a marriage.

The dreaded day arrived. They met with their attorneys inside the courtroom. They divided the belongings I had watched them purchase during happy times. They arranged the custody and visitation for the children.

It was over.

Lindsey had received what she had worked so hard to have, her "freedom" from Casey and the world she had always known. The divorce papers were signed by both parties. All that was left was for the judge to affix his signature to finalize the divorce.

We were at the end of the road, or so it appeared.

Serious Questions

As the miracle I had believed for seemed to be dead, I found myself entering a place I had never been before. Even in prayer, two questions seemed to be coming out of the deepest place of my soul— "Why?" and "Where are You, God?"

Through the years, I had often heard people say we should never ask God, "Why?" But after years of walking in intimacy with Him, I had come to believe, when our questions are coming from a heart of trusting love, it's okay to ask God, "Why?"

Then as only He could do, the Holy Spirit reminded me that even Jesus, in His humanity, had asked those same questions. He led me to Matthew 24:46, "At about three o'clock, Jesus called out with a loud voice, 'Eli, Eli, lema sabachthani?' Which means 'My God, my God, why have you abandoned me?'"

In the hour of His greatest struggle, Jesus too reached a place that went beyond His natural ability to see or understand. When He cried out, "Why?" His question was not met with an immediate answer. It required Him to surrender and trust His Father completely.

"Have you abandoned me?" For me, this was another way of saying, "Where are You?" In that one statement, Jesus had asked both questions—"Why?" and "Where are You?"

I found comfort in knowing, truly, we have a High Priest who is touched by the feelings of our infirmities as Hebrews 4:15 says.

With nothing left but His promises, my anxious eyes looked for the supernatural intervention of my Father. Like a child crying in the darkness, I grasped to feel the nearness of His Presence assuring me that everything was going to be all right.

As the battle ensued, I swung between unspeakable questions and unexplainable peace.

The Final Battle

Several years ago, when Lindsey was much younger, I had a dream. Lindsey and I were on the fourth floor of a very tall sky scraper. That particular floor was like the inside of a very nice department store. She and I were walking around shopping when, suddenly, the building began to topple over as if it were going to collapse onto the ground.

Everything in the store, including Lindsey and me, was rolling on the floor. Right as the building was about to hit the ground, it rose and began to fall toward the opposite direction.

Then everything started rolling the other way. About to hit the ground again, the building rose up once more.

The same sequence of events happened a few more times.

During the dream, Lindsey and I kept rolling around on the floor until I successfully secured my grip to a display table. With everything still in motion, I pulled myself up and cried out authoritatively, "Pillars, stand strong! Pillars, stand strong!"

With that, amazingly, the building stood perfectly upright, still and firm.

Lindsey and I quickly ran out of the building.

For years, I had pondered the meaning of the dream. In December of 2015, I understood.

It was here I began the hardest part of the journey. The battle I had fought for so long seemed to have been centered around the enemy who had attacked and robbed my family. Now, I faced the greatest battle of all—my battle with God.

A darkness was settling in over my very soul. I was beginning to question everything—I mean—everything I had ever believed or even thought I knew of God, His words to me, His will for my life. Overwrought, I wrote:

> *Been up since 4:00 a.m.*
> *Trying to deal with all these thoughts in my mind.*
> *Father . . . where are You?*
> *I'm sorry.*
> *Need help. Like never before.*
> *My thoughts are too hurtful and deep to pen.*
> *I am trusting that You know this and that You will somehow*
> *have mercy on me and help me and answer me.*
> *I am desperate. Desperate.*
> *Beyond.*
>
> *—December 4, 2015*

In the blackest night of my soul, I was scheduled to be part of the wedding of a precious spiritual daughter of mine in Nashville, Tennessee. Although it was a three-hour drive, I chose to drive alone. The thoughts I was thinking didn't need to be shared with anyone.

For hours, I wrestled with questions I had never before asked.

"God, I have believed all these promises of Yours for almost two years now. It appears what I believed, prayed for, hoped for, and declared is not going to happen. Did I not really hear You? How can I deny these words from You and the supernatural way they came?

"Lord, if I did not hear You right on this, then I don't know how to hear You. I don't know how to believe You. I don't know how to trust You.

"If I have misunderstood You on this, then I question everything I've ever believed. I question every time I've ever heard or thought I heard Your Voice on anything."

Like the dream, the very pillars of my faith in God were shaking. I had never known such an intense battle for faith.

The Wedding Note

I arrived for the wedding at the church in downtown Nashville. Mentally and emotionally unable to get out of my car, I sat in the parking lot until I absolutely had to go inside. I honestly didn't know how I could make it through the night of celebration with this overwhelming sadness consuming me.

I gathered my strength and walked into the beautifully decorated sanctuary. I was wearing the same black suit I had on four weeks earlier for my father's funeral. As I approached the seat reserved for me, I slipped my hand inside my coat pocket. To my surprise, I felt something. I pulled it out. It was a folded, white piece of paper.

My heart was warmed when I looked down and saw the penciled handwriting of my then eight-year-old granddaughter Analeise. On the outside of the folded paper, she had written, "I'm sorry about your daddy." It was then I remembered.

When we were at the funeral, during my father's viewing, she had walked up to me and handed me this note. Because I was greeting so many people, I was unable to read it at the time, so I smiled at her and put the paper in my pocket, forgetting I had placed it there—until now.

Standing inside the sanctuary clothed in its wedding attire, in the greatest warfare I had ever known, I opened her note.

With the handwriting, spelling, and faith of a child, she had written, "And God will send a son that will crush the head of the enemy."

Underneath those words, my little warrior had drawn a picture of a big foot crushing the head of a serpent.

Through the obedient heart of a little girl, God had spoken to me. He promised me the head of my enemy was destined for destruction.

There was also the reminder of the promised son.

Yesterday was the hardest that I ever remember.

I've never known a place like it.

Shaken to the core.

Broken.

Seemingly unaware of the Presence of God.

All I could do was cry out, "Why? Where are You?"

The deepest pain I've ever known.

Yet, last night at the wedding, I sensed Him with me.

Came in exhausted, went to bed around 3:00 a.m.

Got up almost 10:00! Thankful for sleep.

Spent all morning in the Word and prayer.

Meditated on a word I received yesterday.

—December 5, 2015

Chapter Twelve

.....

HEADING BACK

Although I usually enjoyed decorating for the season as early as possible, I wasn't looking forward to Christmas 2015. I had to make myself get ready for "the most wonderful time of the year."

Waiting as late as I could, I began the task of pulling out my plastic tubs from storage. They were filled with Christmas carolers and nativity scenes. To my surprise, my heart was warmed as I looked down and read messages I had written to myself after the Christmas of 2014.

A little less than a year before, I had decided to leave myself messages, written in red marker, on duct tape that I stuck on the side of the tubs: "Believing." "Standing for my miracle." "Remember the promise." "I'll recover everything." They were meant to be words of encouragement and short statements of faith.

For the past several years, we had shared our family Christmases in the Millhouse. Christmas had always been one of my favorite times of the year. Since the girls were very small, I had enjoyed going overboard on food, gifts, and decorating. But the past two Christmases were not the same.

Lindsey had been here in body, but the real Lindsey was nowhere to be found. And, since the separation, Casey wasn't able to be at our family Christmas celebrations. I could feel the emptiness in the room without them there.

Instead of the normal Christmas joy and excitement that filled the Millhouse, the atmosphere was tense and heavy. For the sake of my grandchildren, I tried to decorate and make it as happy as possible for them. However, my heart had broken when, last year, Analeise sat on the couch and cried, saying, "This is the saddest Christmas ever."

That year, during this season, I remember telling Lauren the next Christmas would be wonderful because we were believing our family would surely be restored by then. It had given us hope to get through the Christmas of 2014. But now, here we were. Things were not restored. With the passing of time, things hadn't changed. Truth be told, Lindsey was in a worse condition.

We went through the motions of our normal traditions as much as possible for Christmas 2015. We enjoyed Christmas breakfast and opening presents together. Around noon, everyone left to go home. Lindsey left with the girls to drive to Atlanta so they could be with her father. A spiritual son of mine named, Justin, had also joined us, so he and I worked together to begin the great cleanup on this unusually rainy Christmas Day.

At one point, I looked through the window at the creek beside my house. I was raised on this creek my entire life. I knew the patterns of the water. But something didn't look or feel right. It had rained and rained all night and all morning. The creek was surging and churning. I looked at the pasture fence beside my barn and noticed it was nowhere to be seen. It was completely under water.

A fearful concern gripped my heart. Within minutes the water began to wrap around the Millhouse, the barn, and my home. Concerned for our safety, we left the house to find Lauren and Samuel.

A few minutes later, we returned to my home to find Casey and a dear friend, standing in water up to their thighs, pulling my things to safety. The barn and the Millhouse, so beautifully decorated for Christmas, were now standing knee deep in water. Thankfully, by a miracle of God, the water stopped a few inches short of flooding the inside of my home.

It seemed the flood was just more of the raging storm in my life. Amid it all, I felt the strength that comes from the power of God's promise in Isaiah 59:19, "When the enemy comes in like a flood, the Spirit of the Lord will lift up a standard against him" (NKJV).

Missing Home

December 31, 2015 through January 2, 2016, we held our annual Winter Ramp conference. The conference typically drew about five thousand young men and women to encounter the Presence of God. A lot of work, it required "all hands on deck."

Since the conference began in 2001, my two daughters and sons-in-law have been a major part in making it happen—Samuel in administration leadership, Lauren as director of the conference, Casey preaching the opening night, and Lindsey overseeing choreography of Chosen. The thought of another year without Lindsey being there made everything feel so incomplete. One more time, there would be an emptiness at the event that nothing and no one else could fill. I dreaded another year of seeing the hurt on Casey's face as he had to watch all the other ministry leadership couples enjoy the fellowship of being together.

I had to leave in the afternoon of December 31 to drive to Pigeon Forge, Tennessee, where the event was being held. I didn't want to leave without seeing Lindsey, so I invited her to go to lunch with me. Thankfully, she accepted.

As we sat together at one of our local restaurants, I looked across the table at a young woman who looked empty and tired. I said to her, "Lindsey, I want to have a relationship with you. I respect the fact that you are an adult and will make your own decisions with your life. The life you have chosen is a path I have never walked, so I will have to work at understanding how to have the kind of relationship that you want, but I'm willing to try."

Then I asked her a question that I had wondered about, oh, so many times, "Lindsey, do you ever miss us?"

I saw it—a look in her eyes I had not seen for a few years. It was as though she peered through a slit in the door of her cell in the prison I had seen her in, in that one vision. In that brief moment, I saw the eyes of the real Lindsey, and inside those eyes, I saw fear, anger, and great hurt.

"You have no idea how much I have missed a lot of things," she said.

When it was time for me to leave, I drove her back to where her car was parked. As she got out, I said to her, "I've got to head out for Winter Ramp. I sure wish you were going with me."

To my surprise, she said, "I wish I was going, too."

A hopeful hurt swept through me. I wanted to tell her to go get her things right then and get back into my car. But I knew, after all that had happened, she really wasn't ready. Besides, it would have been unfair and unwise to throw her and Casey together at an event where he would be ministering. And then there was the fact that Casey had called me at the beginning of the week, telling me his attorney had called and said the judge would be signing the divorce papers one day that week. Once this was done, everything would be complete, and the divorce would be final.

With nothing left to say, Lindsey and I parted. I drove on to the conference and spent the weekend ministering to thousands of young men and women, while my heart and mind were longing for the one I had left at home.

The Turning Point

I arrived home from Winter Ramp exhausted. It was about 9:00 p.m. I was hungry and decided to fix a sandwich with the intention of going to bed after I finished eating it. I made the sandwich and sat down on the couch when Rick walked into the living room with his phone in his hand.

"I just received a text from Casey." He began to explain, "He took Analeise and Katie back to meet their mother."

I understood per the visitation schedule Casey and Lindsey had worked out that the girls would go with Lindsey after the conference. That meant Casey would take the girls back home and wait until Lindsey picked them up. What I didn't expect was that Lindsey would have someone with her when she went to do so.

"Casey said that Lindsey's new boyfriend drove her to pick up the girls," Rick said. "He had to put the girls in the car seats inside the guy's car." Then, Rick read me the words from Casey's text—words I never wanted to hear.

"It's over. I can't do this anymore. It's time for me to move on."

I put my uneaten sandwich down, picked up my car keys, and walked out the door. Poor Rick, I was so overcome that I left him standing there without any explanation. But he knew me. He understood I had to find God.

I started driving. I wasn't sure where I was going. I needed answers. The glimmer of hope I had felt after lunch with Lindsey was gone. She had said there were "a lot of things" she missed—and now she had been so bold as to put this in Casey's face? I didn't understand.

After an hour or more of driving down the country roads of my city, I ended up parked in the driveway of an empty house on our property. I sat in my car and cried.

What do I do now? After two years of praying every day, after two years of believing these supernatural promises, here we are. It's over? I don't get it!

Looking up at the star-filled midnight sky, I screamed, "Why, God? *Why?!* Why and where are You? *Where—are—You?!* God, I'm not asking where You are because I'm angry at You. You know my heart. I'm asking where You are because I believed You! I believed Your promises."

With tears streaming down my face and my heart broken, I lifted my voice with everything left inside me. With my face turned heavenward, I cried, "Lord, You told Martha that Lazarus was going to live again. *You told her that!* Now, Lord, tell me! Is this marriage going to live again, or is it not? Please answer me! Because if You do not tell me that this marriage is *not* going to live, if You do not tell me that *it is over,* then I am still going to believe everything You've told me!"

Something moved in me. I knew that something also had shifted in Heaven and on Earth.

Then I heard the Voice, "Say out loud, 'Lindsey and Casey are getting back together.'"

When I tried to repeat the statement, I was surprised how deep that hope had been buried inside me. It was literally hard to get it out of my mouth. With what sounded like more of a mumble than a statement, I said halfheartedly, "Lindsey and Casey are getting back together."

"Say it again," the Voice told me.

So, I repeated, "Lindsey and Casey are getting back together."

Again, I was told, "Say it again."

In obedience, I said it again, a bit louder and a bit more confident, "Lindsey and Casey are getting back together."

The Voice and I went back and forth like this a few more times.

Finally, the truth of the statement sunk in, and faith rose up. It was a moment of true revelation. In an instant, I stopped repeating what God had told me to say and began to declare it!

"Lindsey and Casey *are getting back together!*"

Now, I didn't just declare it out of my mouth; I declared it out of my heart. I meant it. No, I *meant* it! I actually *believed* it! Something had shifted. Something was different this time. I believed it, and I *knew* I believed it.

Being so late at night, I had no one I could tell. Everyone was asleep. But I *had* to tell somebody!

I looked beside me and laying there on the passenger seat was my cell phone. I picked it up and began to "pretend" call people. I typed with my index finger in the air over my phone's screen—pretending I was dialing a real number.

Then I held the phone to my ear and said, in a very loud voice, "Hello! Did you hear the incredible news? Lindsey and Casey are getting back together! Yes, it's true! I know! Can you believe it? We are just beside ourselves. Gotta go! Bye!"

Then I pretended to dial someone else, "Hey! It's Karen. Guess what? Lindsey and Casey are getting back together! Of course, we are thrilled! Oh, yes, the girls are so happy. We are all so happy! Gotta go! Bye!"

This continued for some time! I pretended to call a lot of people, declaring what I knew in my heart to be true.

When I pulled out of that driveway to go home, I had a different kind of peace in my heart. It didn't matter to me that the circumstances had reached the end. Biblically, I knew there had to be a death before Lazarus could be raised, and there had to be a "coming to himself" before the prodigal returned to his father. God had told me Lindsey and Casey were getting back together, and I believed it.

The next morning, I awoke with a living hope in my heart. I didn't dare tell anyone else what I had done, not even my husband. He was already too concerned about my mental health by this time anyway, so I didn't want to give him any more reason to wonder or fear!

I knew Pam would understand, though, so I called her and told her what God had said to me. As always, Pam totally agreed and felt the same hope and faith that I did.

Every day that week, we called each other and said, "Did you hear the news? Lindsey and Casey are getting back together!"

Back and forth we would go, as though it were already fully manifested!

One time, Pam said, "Did you hear about the book Lindsey has written on her journey home? It's on the *New York Times* best sellers list!"

"Oh, that's wonderful!" I replied. "I did hear about it!"

The next day, Pam said to me, "I just heard that they are going to be on *Good Morning America,* giving their testimony!"

"Oh, Pam, it's such a miracle. Look what God has done!"

Every day that week, we talked to each other like this. Some people would call us crazy. I say that we were simply being like our Father! We called "those things which do not exist as though they did" (Romans 4:17 NKJV).

Even though the natural circumstances were begging for my attention, there was an unmovable, childlike faith in me that remained. It was an *even now* faith that knew, "God was near."

Chapter Thirteen

COMING DOWN THE DUSTY ROAD

Sunday afternoon, exactly one week since my midnight encounter with God's Voice, Leah came over to help me clean and mop up the mud that had filled the Millhouse from the flood. It had been three weeks since the flood, and we were still cleaning.

As I was putting things back in their place, I heard the familiar *ding* on my phone. Picking it up, I read a text message from Lindsey telling me she was coming over to my house. I was pleasantly surprised and wondered what to expect.

I had experienced hopeful moments like this so many times only to be thrown to the ground in painful disappointment. I left the Millhouse and walked across the yard to my house. I wanted to prepare myself for her arrival. I could sense something was stirring in the atmosphere around me. My heart was trembling with hope and a little fear.

I kept looking out my living room window that overlooks the view from my front porch. This place, this moment seemed to hold all that this journey represented.

I was standing inside the small living room that held within it the prayers of faith and songs of praise of my family before me. Somehow I felt strengthened and encouraged by their witness. It was here in this place my own faith had been established. And it was this deep-rooted faith that had brought me to this very moment when I stood in front of the window, watching the road.

Then I saw it. It was her little white car coming in the distance. I watched as she turned into my driveway and parked in front of my house. Within seconds, her car door opened, and she began to walk down the broken sidewalk my grandfather had placed there to welcome those who wanted to come home.

As she climbed the porch steps, I opened the door to welcome her inside.

"Hello, Honey!"

Wasting no time she replied, "Mom, I want to talk to you."

We walked inside the kitchen and sat down at the table—the same place we had sat two years earlier when she told me her final answer.

With a nervous look on her face, she said, "Mother, I'm going to ask you not to say anything about this to anyone right now, but I just sent this email message to Casey."

She placed her cell phone on the table and slid it toward me.

I picked up her phone and read these words, "Casey, I made the worst mistake of my life divorcing you. I have hurt everybody. I don't deserve a second chance, but I would give up anything to have one. I really can't explain everything that has happened. But this morning I woke up missing you terribly. I truly am sorry."

After I read the email, she said, "I don't know what happened, Mom, but I woke up this morning, and I missed him. I want to come home."

Those words, oh, those words—"I want to come home"—the words I had spent more than two years yearning and longing to hear. All the prayers, tears, and decrees of faith were coming together in this moment, this promised "suddenly" moment! My faith had become sight, and it was sitting right in front of me! I could see it, hear it, touch it! My daughter was coming home!

I looked at her face. The darkness was gone. I looked deeper into those dark blue eyes, and for the first time in three years, I could see her—the real Lindsey. Broken and scared, weary yet hopeful, she was there. She was back!

The defiance seemed to have been shattered and replaced with a broken resolve to do God's will, whatever it would take. The spirit of deception had lost its hold on her. Truth had opened the door of her prison, and she wanted to find her way home.

I wanted to run. I wanted to scream. I wanted to laugh. I wanted to cry.

Instead, I hid my exploding emotions behind the "that is wonderful, Honey," face of a mother who knew she had to let her daughter be in control of the moment. "I'll help you in any way I can," I said as emotionally-controlled as I could with firecrackers and Fourth of July fireworks going off inside me.

I also knew what this meant for Casey. There would be such a myriad of emotions for him to work through. He had been through three years of turmoil, the pain of betrayal, so many lies, and so much hurt. Only God could help and heal his broken heart.

But I also knew what God had told me, "Lindsey and Casey are getting back together." I knew that, not only would God keep His promise, He would also give Casey and Lindsey all the grace and help they would need to walk through the healing and restoration of their marriage.

To my joyful delight, Lindsey did not even want to go back that night to the apartment she had been living in. She wanted to stay at my house! I could tell her heart was daring to hope, and desire was building inside her that Casey would take her back.

Her Return

Once she settled in my upstairs for the night, I found myself alone, sitting on my couch, unable to sleep. This time, though, it was not because of the pain in my soul, but because of the overwhelming joy in my heart!

I wanted to tell somebody. *Pam! Mom! Lauren! I don't care that it's almost midnight. They need to be awake like me! Who can I call?* I wondered, but then I remembered I had given Lindsey my word that I wouldn't tell anyone until *she* had spoken with Casey and our family. I could hardly contain myself. I felt like the parents of the twelve-year-old girl whom Jesus raised from the dead. They had just received their daughter back to life when Jesus told them not to tell anybody.

I have to admit, I didn't break my word, but I did find a little way to at least let Pam know something was going on. I texted her at 11:49, "Pam . . . you up?"

"I am. Are you all right?" she asked

"Yes . . . God is at work," I replied.

"Praise, God! I believe it!" she said.

"Pam, God is here," with that we ended our chat.

Finally, it was morning. I don't know how I made it through that night. I was so grateful to awake and realize the whole thing hadn't been a dream. I heard Lindsey's footsteps coming down the stairs. As she walked into my kitchen, where I was preparing breakfast, I sensed Lindsey was different. The tension, anxiety, and anger she used to bring into any room she was in was now gone. She was changed from the inside out. I just kept staring at this miracle in front of my eyes, trying to take it all in!

As we began to make plans for the day, she actually wanted me to go with her to Florence to pick up some of her things because she didn't want to spend the night at her apartment anymore. I was elated yet still trying to conceal the unspeakable joy and hope that were all up inside me.

Arriving in Florence, we decided to have a quick lunch together. She wanted to eat at Ricatoni's, because she and Casey had eaten there when they were dating. I sat across the table looking into the beautiful face of the daughter I had known; she was back inside her body. She had been returned to me. The darkness that had surrounded her was gone! Her eyes, that had looked so empty, were now filled with light and dancing with life!

To beat the band, all she wanted to talk about was Casey. She kept trying to communicate with him through texts. She sent him a picture of the menu from Ricatoni's, hoping he would remember that their first date was there. She did not know what to expect from him, but I could tell she was willing to try anything.

After our meal, we returned home later that afternoon. I had already planned for the Ramp leadership team to watch the College Football Playoff National Championship in the Millhouse. It was Bama versus Clemson. Knowing that Lindsey was going to be there, Casey chose to watch the game at a friend's house. To my amazement, she left him some snacks on his front porch, a bag of Reese's peanut butter cups and a six-pack of Pepsi with a note about the game.

A few minutes later, Lindsey arrived at the Millhouse. The leadership team had already arrived and were enjoying the food and fellowship. As Lindsey walked through the door, she saw her sister, Lauren, for the first time since her "awakening." Because I kept my word to Lindsey, I had not been able to share with Lauren all that was happening.

Lindsey walked straight to Lauren and Samuel, asking them to step inside the Millhouse pantry with her. It was there that she poured out her heart and asked for their forgiveness. Tears and love flowed out as God brought about the supernatural healing of our family. I was simply in awe of Him.

The next morning, she and I made another trip to Florence to pick up a few more of her things. All the way there, she talked about Casey and played me songs that expressed her hopeful heart.

Finally, she could wait no longer. She sent Casey a text, asking if he would meet with her to talk.

The time had come for her to face the consequences of the decisions she had made. This was the necessary conversation that revealed the truths she had hidden from him for the past three years. There were many questions to be answered and much pain to be processed. For Lindsey, the outcome of that conversation was uncertain. After Casey knew the truth, would he even be willing to take her back?

Everything was at stake.

Everything was hanging on this conversation—on this moment.

His Response

They agreed to meet and talk that night. I was to pick up the girls from Casey's house at nine o'clock so Casey and Lindsey could be alone for the first time since all of this began.

My heart was filled with hope as I pulled into his driveway, walked inside, gave "Grandmother hugs," and quickly began to gather the girls' things. Within minutes, I walked out with two little girls who had no idea their entire future was hanging on what was about to happen inside that house.

I opened the front door and noticed Lindsey had arrived and was sitting in her car at the edge of the yard, waiting for me to leave so the girls would not see her. Not knowing what would happen, she didn't want them to get their hopes up.

As I pulled out, I watched in my rearview mirror as she got out of her car and began walking across his yard toward the front door. I could only imagine what she must have been feeling—the fear of telling him everything that had happened and everything that she'd done, the uncertainty of his reaction, and the hope that somewhere inside him, love and forgiveness for her might still be found.

My heart prayed, *Oh, Father, give her the strength to do this. Give Casey the grace he will need to hear the truth. I am trusting You, Father. I am still standing on every promise You have given me.*

I took the girls to my house and prepared them a late-night snack. As they sat at my kitchen counter, little five-year-old Katie said to me, "My mommy and daddy are getting a divorce, and I don't want them to."

"I'm still believing for a miracle," Analeise quickly responded.

My heart exploded in thought, *Oh, Analeise, if you only knew what was going on RIGHT NOW! Keep believing, Honey! Keep believing!*

I sat up most of the night waiting on Lindsey to come home. Waiting and waiting. Watching the clock. Walking the floor. Wondering and wondering what was going on.

I wanted to drive to the house to see if her car was still there, but I couldn't leave the girls! *How is it going? Could they still be talking? Is this a good sign or a bad sign?*

Either way, I was still believing the Word. I tried to calm myself with the thought that this is just the first of many conversations to come. I figured it would probably take several months for them to work through all that had happened. They would probably start to "date" again and then go to counseling. It didn't matter to me what it took. I just wanted to see my daughter fully healed and her marriage and home restored.

It was now getting into the morning hours, 2:00 a.m., 4:00 a.m—still no word from them.

Walking the floor, sitting on the couch, getting up again, watching the second hand on the living room clock, *ticking, ticking.* I had to fight off fear as I wondered if she had gotten upset, left his house, and was out driving somewhere.

I finally drifted off to sleep for a quick nap.

Ding. It was 7:30 a.m. I looked at my phone. It was Lindsey letting me know she was on her way back from meeting with Casey.

My heart leapt! They were still together! She had never left his house. Surely, this had to mean something wonderful!

A few minutes later, Lindsey pulled into my driveway, driving Casey's jeep! When she got out, I noticed she was wearing Casey's sweatshirt. It took everything in me to act nonchalant. Inside, I wanted to start running through the yard, dancing like a fool!

I managed to collect my emotions and ask, "How did it go, Lindsey?"

With a radiant smile on her face, she replied, "Well, we talked all night. It was the hardest thing I've ever done in my life. I told him everything. The conversation was intense. Very intense. We talked and cried until there was nothing left in either of us. But, Mother, when I picked up my keys to go, he told me he didn't want me to leave. He wanted me to stay."

And she never left again.

Home to Stay

Lindsey is home. She is whole. Her joy, her identity, and her beauty have been restored. Casey and Lindsey's marriage is restored.

Analeise and Katie saw the power of God answer their prayers.

On December 1, 2016, two years to *the exact day* that God gave me the promise, "You will hold a son in your arms," Casey Asher Huck Doss was born! The son of promise. The son of restoration.

Just as He promised, God came. He fully kept His promises to me.

In fact, God kept *every* promise He had made me. Every—single— one.

God did in a moment what would have taken twenty years of counseling. The captive of the warrior *was released*! The plunder of the tyrant was *retrieved*!

I surely recovered *everything* that was taken from me. There was a supernatural turnaround! It was as *easy as a feather,* and the wall came crashing down!

A lot happened in *three days*! On January 10, 2016, Lindsey woke up, wanted to come home, and sent the email to Casey. On January 11, she was restored to her family. On January 12, she met with Casey for full restoration.

And did you notice the date in the middle? 1/11. That's right, 111! God's final answer was "marriage. Period."

God had done what no man could do. He gave Lindsey the grace to come to Casey in full repentance and truth, and He gave Casey the grace to love and forgive her.

Chapter Fourteen

.....

THE LAST WORD

My dear friend,

I want to encourage your faith to keep believing for the one you love to return home.

I believe your sons and daughters were in that throng of freed ones that was following Lindsey out of the house of bondage! I believe that is why you are holding this book in your hands! God wanted to give you a Word to hold on to so that you will know and believe, there is no one and nothing too hard for our God!

One word from God is enough. Just one word can move any mountain and destroy any foe. One word from God is enough to carry you through the rest of your life! But, as you have read in my story, in His kindness and mercy, He will give you as many words as you need to hear. Jesus said for us to pray, "Give us this day our *daily* bread." He will give you two pieces of bread on the same day if that's what you need! How good is our Father?!

Things don't have to stay the way they have been and are. You don't have to sit back and allow the enemy to destroy your life and those you love. You don't have to find a way to move on with your life! You don't have to accept anything that is not your Father's will.

You are on the earth to be an ambassador of Heaven. You are the one the Father has found while searching throughout the earth for a conduit of faith through which He can release His will.

Prayerfully determine what God has to say about your situation. Then become the intercessor who stands in the gap between the circumstance and the promise until the circumstance is conformed to His will!

Your loved one may not be speaking to you right now. He may spit in your face and tell you he hates you. You may have to stand there and be the object of his resentful scorn as he screams, "It's none of your business where I go and what I do. I'm an adult! I can make my own decisions. Stop trying to control me!"

This battle of words can feel like a knife piercing your very soul. The pain can cut so deeply that you feel tempted to build a wall around your heart so that you never feel pain like this again.

Or maybe you've already promised yourself that you will somehow learn to live without a deep relationship with the one you love, thinking, *She can live her life, and I will live my life.*

At this point, you may be overcome and want off the emotional roller coaster, convincing yourself it's time to lay it all down and give up.

But you can't do that. Don't give up. Not now. Not later. I'm here to tell you that your prayers are working. God is not a respecter of persons. What He has done for me and for so many others, He can do for you. I'm convinced of it!

Today is the day of your deliverance! Don't look at the circumstances—look to your promises, and keep watching the road!

You've read my story. You've seen how faithful the Father was to speak to me, to use others to encourage me. But I want to remind you today that He wants to speak to you, He is speaking to you, and He has a plan for your good and not for evil. He has a special strategy to give you. It's something I learned in the very beginning of my journey, but I wanted to wait until after you heard the whole story before I shared it with you, because now is when you're going to need it.

During my season of intercession, I made a new "old" friend. His name was Jehoshaphat. He taught me a battle strategy that worked for him. It has worked for me, and I believe it will work for you as well.

Jehoshaphat faced a situation that was urgent, impossible, and completely overwhelming. I was drawn to his story in 2 Chronicles 20:1–30. Let's look at the beginning together. We read,

> *After this, the armies of the Moabites, Ammonites, and some of the Meunites declared war on Jehoshaphat, "A vast army from Edom is marching against you from beyond the Dead Sea."*
>
> *—2 Chronicles 20:1–2*

Jehoshaphat was not facing just one enemy but three—and at the same time! Have you ever felt like you were being hit from several directions at once? You're dealing with a wayward child, your marriage is in shambles, a financial crisis has hit you, and the doctor tells you some bad news.

Like Jehoshaphat, we too are at war. However, our war is not fought against natural enemies. As we read in Ephesians 6:12, we are fighting against "evil rulers and authorities of the unseen world, against mighty powers in this dark world."

When you realize you are in a spiritual battle for the freedom of someone you love and, like Jehoshaphat, you are surrounded on several fronts, that does not mean it is time to give up and throw in the proverbial towel! It means you get up and start tightening up your armor. It's time to fight.

Thankfully, we are not left defenseless against these adversaries who seek to destroy our lives and families. God has clearly laid out a battle plan for our victory. Jehoshaphat shows us what we must do.

The Weapon of Fasting

Fasting was the first thing Jehoshaphat did. In 2 Chronicles 20:3, we read, "Jehoshaphat was terrified by this news and begged the Lord for guidance. He also ordered everyone in Judah to begin fasting." This became a real strategy for me in my daughter's deliverance.

As I shared with you in Chapter 5, I do not enjoy fasting. Everything in me wants to cave in to my flesh, but I found it to be an effective weapon. It made me press into God and rely upon Him to sustain me.

Set your heart to make fasting part of your intercessory journey. There are many different kinds of fasts. You may fast a meal or two a day. You may do a Daniel fast by not eating meats or sweets. You may even fast on a particular day each week for so many weeks. Whichever fast you undertake, make the fast count. Use the sacrifice to press into God.

I believe God is moved when we sacrifice anything for the purpose of saying to Him, "God, I want You more." He honors our seeking hearts and keeps His promise that, when we hunger and thirst, we shall be filled.

The Weapon of Prayer

The second thing Jehoshaphat did was, He *prayed*:

> *Jehoshaphat stood before the community of Judah and Jerusalem in front of the new courtyard at the Temple of the Lord. He prayed, "O Lord, God of our ancestors, you alone are the God who is in heaven. You are ruler of all the kingdoms of the earth. You are powerful and mighty; no one can stand against you! O our God. . . . We are powerless against this mighty*

*army that is about to attack us. We do not know what to do,
but we are looking to you for help."*

—*2 Chronicles 20:5–12*

I don't believe this was just a nice, half-hearted, devotional prayer. Jehoshaphat knew—for his family, his people, and him—it was a matter of life or death. He and all Israel stood together in perfect agreement and prayed with all their hearts. I love the statement and have used it often in prayer myself, "I don't know what to do, but my eyes are on You."

It's nice and fine to ask other people to pray for you, but no one can pray about your situation like you can. *You* pray! And don't pray pretty little prayers. Those are nice in their place, but when you are desperate, learn how to pray faith-filled, desperate prayers!

Pray with all *your heart.* Jeremiah 29:13 says, "You will seek me and find me when you seek me with all of your heart!" Pray with such hunger and desire that it involves everything in your body, your soul (mind, will, and emotions), and your spirit. This is a glorious experience!

Pray loud sometimes. Go somewhere no one else can hear you, and call out to God with everything in your being! You may feel awkward at first, but do it anyway because Jesus prayed this way. Hebrews 5:7 says, "While Jesus was here on earth, he offered prayers and pleadings, with a *loud* cry and tears, to the one who could rescue him from death. And God heard his prayers because of his deep reverence for God."

Pray with deep passion and emotion, telling God every concern of your heart. If you're afraid, tell Him you're afraid. If you're angry, tell Him you're angry. If you're hurt and offended, tell Him! He knows anyway, but He loves to hear you acknowledge your dependence on Him. He wants to know that you are going nowhere else for healing and direction.

Pray in the Spirit by praying in other tongues. There are times when we have prayed everything we know to pray. We have done everything we know to do, and the problem is still there and getting worse by the day. There are times when the pain is so deep that there are no words for prayer. This is when we allow the Holy Spirit to pray for us.

Romans 8:26–27 says,

> *And the Holy Spirit helps us in our weakness. For example, we don't know what God wants us to pray for. But the Holy Spirit prays for us with groaning that cannot be expressed in words. And the Father who knows all hearts knows what the Spirit is saying, for the Spirit pleads for us believers in harmony with God's own will.*

This is so amazing! I've said it before, but it bears repeating: *The Holy Spirit is our prayer partner!* When we have no understanding and have exhausted our ability, the Spirit steps in and prays through us the perfect will of the Father. When our pain finds no expression in human language, when our sorrow turns to nothing but a wordless moan, the precious Holy Spirit takes our deepest groan and turns it into a prayer that the Father understands, hears, and answers!

Change your posture in prayer. Instead of sitting comfortably in your favorite chair with your coffee close at hand, step out and do something different. Walk. March. Lie down. Crawl. Run. Kneel. Shout. Sing. Stomp. I was so desperate to hear from God and see a breakthrough for my daughter that I assumed all these approaches and more. Do what the Holy Spirit tells you to do. That's what you do!

Change your place of prayer. Do you have a favorite place to pray? That's wonderful, but on this prayer journey, I found it was good for me to step outside my comfort zone. I prayed throughout the house, in the yard, driving down the road, parked in a random church parking lot, and stomping around on my front porch. I prayed in the Ramp. I borrowed the key to the church I was raised in as a child to go pray there at random times throughout the night. I prayed walking down "the old dirt road" that runs behind my house. When I had to go shop at Walmart, I didn't want to miss my time in prayer, so I walked down the grocery aisle, holding my cell phone to my ear, talking to God about Lindsey as though He were listening on the other end of the phone, because He was.

Pray until you "pray through." I was raised in a wonderful, traditional Pentecostal church called, *The Church of God of Prophecy.* In our church, we experienced what the old folks called, "praying through." This form of prayer involves continuing to pray until you sense yourself breaking through the earthly realm into the spiritual realm where you can lose all sense of time and space. Paul described one of these experiences by saying, "God only knows whether I was in my body or outside my body" (2 Corinthians 12:3).

A mighty woman of God, whom I greatly respect, by the name of Martha Tennison described praying through like this, "You pray until you touch Heaven. And you *keep* praying until Heaven touches you."

I learned to pray this way as a child, because this is the way I heard my mother pray. Oh, how well I remember the sound of her voice filling our house as she prayed.

I can remember at night, when my father and sister and I were already in bed, hearing my mother praying from the living room. I would slip out of bed, walk down the hallway, and peek into the living room. There she would be, kneeling beside the couch, calling on God. There were many nights I would slip under her arm as she knelt there and go to sleep with the sound of her voice and her passion for prayer soaking into my spirit. I cherish those memories!

I'm not saying we have to pray loud and aggressive every time we pray. I understand there are many forms of prayer, and I love them all!

There are many, many times I have a wonderful, intimate experience with Jesus in the quiet gentleness of prayer. But I believe we are well-practiced in that form of prayer. I think we need to be encouraged more to get out of our comfort zone a bit and pray mighty prayers to our Mighty God!

The Weapon of the Word

We know that Jehoshaphat fasted and prayed. Then, in 2 Chronicles 20:13–17, we read what happened next:

> *As the men of Judah stood before the Lord with their little ones, wives, and children, the Spirit of the Lord came upon one of the men standing there. His name was Jahaziel . . . . He said, "Listen, all you people of Judah and Jerusalem! Listen, King Jehoshaphat! This is what the Lord says: Do not be afraid! Don't be discouraged by this mighty army, the battle is not yours, but God's. Tomorrow, march out against them. You will find them coming up through the ascent of Ziz at the end of the valley that opens into the wilderness of Jeruel. But you will not even need to fight. Take your positions; then stand still and watch the Lord's victory. He is with you, O people of Judah and Jerusalem. Do not be afraid or discouraged. Go out against them tomorrow, for the Lord is with you!"*

Oh, how awesome! Jehoshaphat prayed, and God answered!

Pray until you hear a word from God! He *will* speak to you. He *wants* to speak to you! He *will* speak loud, clear, and often. That's the one thing I hope my testimony demonstrated—proved—to you!

And know this, too, God knows how to speak to you in ways that only you will understand. This is so you will be assured that you have indeed heard from Him, so that there will be no doubt about it. That is the kind of word you can cling to, the kind of word you can believe and stand on.

Start looking for His response. The expressions of the Voice are amazing, wonderful, and endless. You read the many ways I heard His Voice—via texts from friends, in casual conversations, and His Word jumping off the page. I heard His Voice in songs being played on the radio as I was shopping. He spoke to me through movies. He spoke to me and others in night dreams, encouraging me to believe that Lindsey was coming home. He spoke to me through creation and nature. In fact, God spoke to me in more ways than I could even mention.

My friend Cindy has a special love for "red birds." God knows that about her, and so many times He will use a little red bird to get her attention and remind her of His love or promise.

How can you hear the Voice? Keep your heart full of expectancy, your eyes *always* searching, and your ears sensitive and *constantly* open to His gentle whispers or His loud roar.

In 2 Peter 1:4, Peter calls the promises of God "exceeding great and precious." Once you receive a word from God, go ahead and make a big deal out of it. Write it down immediately. You may think you'll remember it, but most likely you won't. Write it down in your journal. Write it on a sticky note and put it on your mirror. Make it the screen saver on your computer or cell phone. Tape it to the dash of your car. I have a spiritual daughter named Stacie who writes her words on white butcher paper that's several feet long. She hangs it on the wall of her house. Whatever that looks like for you, just keep that word in front of your face!

I took the words God gave me and wrote many of them on index cards to keep in my Bible. The stack grew thicker and thicker, as His precious promises kept coming. These promises were how I built a strong arsenal of weapons against the enemy. When I was in prayer, I would take out my index cards and read them aloud (sometimes, very loudly). I used them as a weapon in my hand until the paper itself became worn. Over and over, I read them and declared the power of the promises into the spiritual atmosphere. The enemy has no weapon to use against the power of God's Word. Remember, God's Word is the final answer!

The Weapon of Believing

Jehoshaphat fasted, prayed, heard a word, and then he believed the word!

> *Early the next morning the army of Judah went out into the wilderness of Tekoa. On the way Jehoshaphat stopped and said, "Listen to me, all you people of Judah and Jerusalem! Believe in the Lord your God, and you will be able to stand firm! Believe in His prophets, and you will succeed."*
> *—2 Chronicles 20:20*

The most important part of receiving a word from God is believing the word from God! Usually, when God speaks, His word will look and sound completely opposite of what we are seeing and hearing.

The circumstance says, "Divorce."

God says, "Marriage."

The circumstance says, "No money,"

God says, "No lack."

The circumstance says, "Sickness."

God says, "Healing."

Now, we have come to the greatest battle of all—believing what you see versus believing what He says.

I remember this day when I asked God, "How do I believe?"

He answered me, "What you meditate on is what you believe."

If we spend our time meditating on the impossibility of the circumstance, we will believe the impossibility of the circumstance.

If we meditate on what God has said about it, we will believe what God has said about it. We will believe that nothing is impossible with Him.

If we talk with our friends and family about how terrible everything looks and how hopeless we feel, we are strengthening our doubt that things will ever change.

However, if we tell our friends and family what God has said about the matter, we are strengthening our faith, because we are hearing the Word come out of our own mouths! And faith comes by "hearing" the Word of God!

To believe the Word of God instead of what you see will require you to change the way you think! It is the natural man in us who is moved and led by our senses. It is easier to think this way because it requires no effort on our part. We just succumb to the circumstances around us and become a slave to fear.

To believe what God says will require us to put forth an effort to fight! Thankfully, we are not in this fight alone. God has equipped us to fight the good fight of faith and win!

Anyone can do this. It is not just for people known to have a "Word of Faith" ministry or those who have a particular personality or spiritual pedigree. God has given to *every* man the measure of faith. And it only takes faith the size of a small mustard seed to move a mountain!

Once you have received a word of promise from God, don't be surprised or moved if the circumstance gets worse instead of better. You will find this to be the case sometimes as the word in you is being tested.

James 1:2 says,

Dear brothers and sisters, when trouble comes your way, consider it an opportunity for great joy. For you know that when your faith is tested, your endurance has a chance to grow. So let it grow, for when your endurance is fully developed, you will be perfect and complete, needing nothing.

James is telling us, when things are going from bad to worse, when God has not delivered you and He has not answered your prayer yet, consider it great joy! Then he tells us, when this is happening, you can be assured God is working something inside you that is more important to Him than your immediate deliverance and answer to prayer.

Now, don't think James is saying God isn't going to answer your prayer by that statement. He's just saying that, while God delights in responding to you with a great deliverance, there is something that is of even more importance to Him: the building of your faith, the strengthening of your endurance, and the development of your character.

So, when the time of your deliverance comes, you will not only receive what you have been praying and believing for, you will be a different person when you come out. Your faith will be strengthened to move even greater mountains. And you will have a testimony to share with the world!

The Weapon of Obedience

Now, after he had fasted, prayed, received a word, and believed the word, Jehoshaphat taught us another step that is critical to our battle strategy. We must *obey* the word we have heard. To understand this more clearly, let's look once more at 2 Chronicles 20:13–17.

> *As the men of Judah stood before the Lord with their little*
> *ones, wives, and children, the Spirit of the Lord came upon*
> *one of the men standing there. His name was Jahaziel . . . .*
> *He said, "Listen, all you people of Judah and Jerusalem! Lis-*
> *ten, King Jehoshaphat! This is what the Lord says: Do not be*
> *afraid! Don't be discouraged by this mighty army, the battle is*
> *not yours, but God's. Tomorrow, march out against them. You*
> *will find them coming up through the ascent of Ziz at the end*
> *of the valley that opens into the wilderness of Jeruel. But you*
> *will not even need to fight. Take your positions; then stand*
> *still and watch the Lord's victory. He is with you, O people of*
> *Judah and Jerusalem. Do not be afraid or discouraged. Go out*
> *against them tomorrow, for the Lord is with you!"*

How wonderful! Jehoshaphat prayed, and God answered. Contained in His answer was His will and strategy. And what a strategy it was!

First of all, God pulled the curtain on exactly where the enemy was and where he was going. I love that! The enemy cannot hide from God. The enemy has no secrets or surprise attacks that are unknown to God. If we will seek Him and listen, as Jehoshaphat did, the Lord will expose satan's plans and strategies to us, and then give us His instructions for a sure victory.

God laid out His battle plan for Jehoshaphat. In essence, this was it. March out against them, take your positions, stand still, and watch.

If I had been out there leading the people instead of Jehoshaphat, I would have been thinking, *Now, wait a minute. Did I hear You right? Are You aware that there are three armies coming directly toward us? Just so You know, we are already doing all we know to get ready. I've got my men gathering every weapon and able-bodied man in this country. They are sharpening every sword and arrow we have. The women are polishing shields and making war clothes. If You are with us, we can fight . . . just so You know.*

But God had clearly stated to Jehoshaphat and the children of Israel that they were not going to have to fight in this one. "The battle is not yours, but God's!"

At face value, that sounds like an easy plan for Jehoshaphat to execute. Just stand still and watch. That's it. That's the plan. That's the strategy. "Stand still" and keep your eyes on God. This is easy only if you are on the sidelines watching. If you are on the frontline, staring at a fully armed, massive enemy army advancing directly toward you, standing still and watching a God you cannot see would require a trust that consumes every fiber of your being! Talk about utter dependence on God! Either you've heard from God, or you and your family and friends are all going to die!

Most of the time, when we hear about Jehoshaphat's battle, we hear how the worshippers and singers led them all into battle. I find it interesting that it wasn't God's idea to advance toward the enemy while singing songs of worship. That was Jehoshaphat's idea. He knew what the children of Israel were about to see. He knew the heart of man would wax fearful. In this battle, fear would cost them everything. So, he came up with a plan:

> *Early the next morning the army of Judah went out into the wilderness of Tekoa. On the way, Jehoshaphat stopped and said, "Listen to me, all you people of Judah and Jerusalem! Believe in the Lord our God, and you will be able to stand firm. Believe in his prophets and you will succeed." After consulting the people, the king appointed singers to walk ahead of the army, singing to the Lord and praising him for his holy splendor. This is what they sang: "Give thanks to the Lord, His faithful love endures forever!"*
>
> *—2 Chronicles 20:20–21*

To the children of Israel, it looked like a flesh-and-blood battle, after all the only thing the natural eye could see were fully armed, screaming warriors running toward them. But according to the "Word" they had heard, it was a spiritual war. It was going to be fought for them in the spirit realm. It was God's battle, not theirs. Jehoshaphat knew that, if they were distracted by what their natural eyes saw and their natural ears heard, it was over.

So, how do you fight a spiritual battle? How do you trust that God is going to fight for you? Like Jehoshaphat, you do what God tells you. You stand still and watch Him. Instead of looking at what is coming toward you, you lift up your eyes and set your expectant gaze on Him.

Instead of listening to the roar of the enemy, you lift up your own roar but not toward the enemy. You lift up your roar of worship to God! You sing. Yes, you sing loud and with all your might, "Praise the Lord, His mercy endures forever! Praise the Lord, His mercy endures forever!"

What happened next is amazing! Second Chronicles 20:22–24 says,

> *At the very moment they began to sing and give praise, the Lord caused the armies of Ammon, Moab, and Mount Seir to start fighting among themselves! . . . So when the army of Judah arrived at the lookout point in the wilderness, all they saw were dead bodies lying on the ground as far as they could see. Not a single one of the enemy had escaped.*

Can you imagine the sight they saw? All the bodies of their enemy littered the landscape, as far as they could see! Unreal!

They wouldn't have known this, however, if they didn't do something very important: They went to the "lookout point."

The Weapon of Watching

When they did all that they were told to do, Jehoshaphat and the children of Israel went to the place from which they could see what was going on. They went to the "lookout point in the wilderness."

While you have been praying, while you've been interceding, something has been going on. The Father has confused the enemy, and the enemy's camp is in an uproar.

Father is calling you, even now, to a place, to a position. He wants you to go to your lookout point—to return to your front porch. From there, He wants you to see that He has defeated the enemy who has sought to take out your loved one, to destroy him or her, and to crush your faith in the process. But Father says to return to your watch.

Front porches are the homeplace of intercessors. Everyday they live there, standing in the gap between judgment and mercy, keeping their post on the bridge between the cold, harsh conditions of the fallen world and the love and warmth inside the Father's house. It is from this vantage point they can call the prodigal to come back to God and keep their expectant eyes watching for any sign of hope.

Even when there is no reason for hope, keep hoping. Be like Abraham of old who "never wavered in believing God's promise. In fact, his faith grew stronger, and in this he brought glory to God. He was fully convinced that *God is able to do what He has promised!*" (Romans 4:18–20).

Even if there is no reason for you to hope, when you have a word from God, *there is hope.* Whether your loved one has just left or has been gone for months or years, stay on the porch and don't take your eyes off the road! If he didn't come today or if she hasn't contacted you in months, keep declaring, "Today is the day of deliverance!"

The enemy will send you reports from their place of bondage. Don't believe them. They are lies. The only thing that is true are the promises from your Father.

The worsening circumstances do not change one word God has said to you. The reports you hear are the enemy's attempt to make you give up and stop praying. You can't stop. Even if you go to your grave before you see the manifestation of your promise, then go to your grave *believing!* Your faith and your prayers will remain in effect long after your spirit has left this earthly realm. God will keep the promises He gave you! God's Word *will* come to pass.

But remember, His promises are only activated by faith! Hebrews 11:1 says, "Faith is the substance of things *hoped* for, the evidence of things *not seen.*"

Sometimes hope hurts. When you have gotten your hope up, only to have it violently thrown to the ground over and over, you want to protect your heart from hoping again. You may say, "My eyes are weary from the strain of watching the road day after day, only to see nothing, nothing. I've been camping here on this porch of intercession for years, and my heart cannot take the pain of the disappointment anymore."

There are days it would be easier to pack up your things, go back inside to a safe place, and throw hope to the wind. But remember, the prodigal son's father would never have seen his son coming had he not kept watching the road. The day eventually came when his tried faith became sight:

> *The son got up and went to his father. While he was yet a long way off, his father saw him. The father was full of loving-pity for him. He ran and threw his arms around him and kissed him.*
>
> *—Luke 15:20*

I'm so glad Jesus told us what the father did when he finally saw the silhouette of his son coming at a far distance—"he ran"! Without a moment of hesitation, he started running toward the one he loved.

As he ran, tears were flowing as overwhelming joy was bursting in his heart. With every stride, his lips were expressing the song of his heart, "That's my son. My son is coming home. He was dead, but now he's alive! He was lost, but now he is found!"

My dear friend, keep your eyes on the road and get ready to *run!*

ABOUT THE AUTHOR

· · · · · · · ·

Karen Wheaton is a seasoned Christian minister whose music and preaching have provoked listeners to pursue God in passionate worship. She has given her life for the vision and mission of awakening. She continues to travel and minister, but her efforts are primarily focused at the Ramp in Hamilton, Alabama, where thousands gather each year to be transformed by the Presence of God and equipped to win their cities. Karen and her husband, Rick, are laying down their lives to see a generation awakened. Believing for revival in the nations of the earth, they are passionately pursuing the dreams of God.

 facebook.com/karenannwheaton

 instagram.com/karenannwheaton

 youtube.com/TheRampMedia

HAVE YOU EVER WONDERED WHAT IS HAPPENING IN THE MIND AND HEART OF YOUR PRODIGAL? THROUGH THE EYES OF LINDSEY, EXPERIENCE HER JOURNEY AS SHE FINDS THE WAY HOME.